$$$$$$$$$$$

Estate Planning

&

Living Trust

Secrets

$$

What They

Don't Want

You To

Know

By   Frank J. Croke

Capital Management Press
A division of Carolina Capital Management, Inc.
Wilmington, North Carolina 28403

Copyright © 2001 Capital Management Press
Cover Art © 2001 Capital Management Press
Illustrations © 2001 Capital Management Press

Cover design: Mary Croke
Text Design: Mary Croke
Illustrations: Howard Munce

Library of Congress Cataloging-in-Publication Data

Croke, Frank J., 1928-
        Estate Planning & Living Trust Secrets: What They
        Don't Want You to Know / by Frank J. Croke
            p.   cm.
        ISBN 1-892879-30-1 (pbk.)
        1. Living trusts--United States--Popular works.   2. Estate
            planning--United States--Popular works.

                        CIP   Being Issued

This book may be ordered by mail from the publisher.
Please include $3.00 for postage and handling. *But try your bookstore first.*
This publication is available for bulk purchase.
Capital Management Press Publishers
A division of Carolina Capital Management, Inc.
Post Office Box 5905, Wilmington, North Carolina

This publication is designed to provide accurate and authoritative information in regard to the subject matter covered. It is sold with the understanding that the publisher is not, by virtue of distributing this publication, engaged in rendering legal, accounting or other professional service. If legal advice or other expert assistance is required, the services of a competent professional person should be sought. *Adapted from a Declaration of Principles jointly adopted by a Committee of the American Bar Association and a Committee of Publishers and Associations.*

Table of Contents

Table of Contents

Table of Contents

Table of Contents

A TRUST SHOULD BE TAILORED
TO THE NEEDS OF YOUR FAMILY

What They Don't Want
You to Know

Your rights are missing from estate plans

Your Estate Plan should be tailored to your wishes and the needs of your family. These are your rights but they are rarely considered in most estate planning documents. And, since most estate plans fail to specifically state these grantor rights, Default Rules control what happens to your assets. Your document, as it is currently written, is probably inadequate.

As an example, if you are married and the intention of your estate plan is to provide for your spouse and children, you have the right to plan and give directives that will properly accomplish that. Your written directives will not only override the state "Default Rules"but can also help maintain strong family relationships

Boilerplate provisions are in your Trust

They do not want you to know that boilerplate provisions have been used in your documents, such as the method for determining the most important aspect of the Trust: the annual income your surviving spouse will receive. Most Trusts state:

> "My trustee is to pay my surviving spouse
>   the net income from my trust."

The above boilerplate provision in a Trust provides a guarantee nobody wants. It means the surviving spouse - generally the wife - will receive about half the income she needed, half of what she could have received, if the document was properly prepared.

To provide the income the surviving spouse will need and can receive, see Chapter 7.

State "Default Rules" control most estate plans.

They do not tell you that state "Default Rules" will control your Trust. They do not tell you that your document does not give specific directives to properly provide for your family and heirs. Because you are unaware of that, you also don't know the negative financial impact it causes.

You have options, but they were not offered. And because they were not offered, you did not use them. You lost that right.

The state "Default Rules" also determine many of the things your trustee must do but that are not clearly stated in your document. You probably were not told this either.

Many of these documents are so ineffective, it is like dying without a Will. We all know that if we die without a Will the laws of our state will determine how our assets are to be divided, who gets what and when. And, court appointed administrators will take control of our estate.

Basically that same thing happens even though the well-intentioned deceased paid thousands of dollars for a plan they thought was going to do good things. But, unfortunately, their Living Trust or Will contained boilerplate generalities for many important and specific issues that will affect their surviving spouse, their children and their other heirs. And, these well-intentioned grantors knowingly or unknowingly, settled for a lot less than they paid for.

Deceased grantors never realized that they had these options and many who are not deceased don't know it either. Persons who prepared such documents never informed the grantors of their rights. Why? The material that follows will offer some answers.

Your key options are not taught in law schools

Most people assume that topics so important as their basic rights in estate planning are taught in law schools. But this is not so. And, who has ever had someone in the legal profession tell you this?

The major options a grantor has in estate planning are not yet taught in most law schools. Law schools teach general concepts and history of law. Law school courses in estate planning need to ad key grantor financial and management options to the required course of study.   The rights of grantors must be presented. Most of these rights concern financial and management issues - an area in which many attorneys have limited knowledge and experience.

Lawyers lose their malpractice coverage if they give the advice you need

One would expect that if you went to a Trust attorney for assistance in your estate plan, you would be properly advised on your rights and your key options.

These are rights and options you need to exercise if you are serious about properly providing for your family. Most of your key options in estate planning are financial and investment directives.

However, many insurance policies clearly state that an attorney can lose his malpractice coverage if he or she gives investment advice.

Lawyers Mutual, a company that insures about 80% of the attorneys in North Carolina, has this restriction in the policies it issues as do many other insurance carriers. And, they don't want you to know it.

Board Certified Specialists in Estate Planning

To make matters worse, some states are certifying attorneys as specialists in estate planning. The concept of specialization on legal issues has been picked up from the medical profession. If doctors are "Board Certified" in their specialty such as brain surgery or heart transplants, the public knows that these doctors have spent years achieving the skills. And, these medical specialist earn the high fees they receive for their work.

Attorneys decided to apply this concept of certification to the legal profession. Many are now party to this. Attorneys are "Board Certified as Specialist in Wills, Trusts and Estate Planning." But there is a difference between the medical community and the legal community and it is a matter of standards and degree of skill required for certification.

States give certification without requiring that

the attorney be properly trained and tested in their knowledge of the most important financial and management options a person has in their estate plans.

These "Board Certified Specialists in Estate Planning" are not tested nor required to know any of your rights and key options to place into your document to properly provide for and protect your family. But you are never told nor do they want you to know that

Some law schools are now giving this certification based on courses taken, but without including the vital knowledge of the key options we will discuss in this book.

A deceptive practice by the legal profession

States that grant such false "certifications" that then permit attorneys to advertise this bogus certification to prospective clients are perpetrating a deceptive practice against their citizens. And for the legal profession to willingly continue this deception reflects a good deal more than poor judgement. Fraudulent activity, no matter how respectable the appearance, eventually is exposed.

I have reviewed for many clients Trusts prepared by "Board Certified Specialists in Estate Planning." All of these clients quickly saw that key issues were missing from their plans and understood that they needed to revise their original documents. All were annoyed and justifiably felt deceived.

These were influential people, who had held responsible positions, had accumulated a fair amount of assets and were active in their communities. The services they received on their original documents reflects poorly on the entire legal profession, that unfortunately includes many fine attorneys who work for the best interest of their clients. Good attorneys are being needlessly harmed by these false certifications of others. Greedy attorneys use invalid certification to justify their higher fees.

The conferring of this empty and meaningless title should be stopped. But the political structure in the legal community makes it difficult to correct.

Good Trust attorneys may be able to claim they are a specialists in taxation and the laws of probate and be so certified after fulfilling stringent requirements. But, tax law is only one small part of estate planning. Attorneys should not be certified as specialists in estate planning without substantial changes being made in the curriculum in law schools, changes that require financial training and new procedures for testing candidates for certification in estate planning.

Canons of legal ethics violated

States have professional codes or canons for attorneys. These are state rules an attorney must follow. A rule common to all states is the role of an attorney as an advisor. This rule states:

"In representing a client, a lawyer shall exercise independent professional judgement and render candid advice. In rendering advice, a lawyer may refer not only to the law, but also to other considerations such as moral, economic, social and political factors that may be relevant to the client's situation.

The lawyers responsibility as advisor may include indicating that more may be involved than strictly legal considerations.

Matters that go beyond strictly legal considerations may also be in the domain of other professions. . . Where consultation with a professional in another field is itself something a competent attorney would recommend, the lawyer should make such a recommendation."

There are some Trust attorneys who advise a grantor on their financial and management options contained in this book. But, many who do not, also fail to recommend a grantor's need to consult with a person who could give advice on financial rights to consider for an estate plan.

My work of reviewing Trusts would not be required if grantors had been advised to seek consultation with highly qualified professionals.

When grantors are not so advised by their attorney, cannons of legal ethics are being ignored

They do not want you to know that you should have been advised to seek consultation with highly qualified financial planners, CPAs, or other professionals trained in grantor options in estate planning.

The Legal Profession is not properly serving clients in estate planning- a summary

First, law schools ignore these financial and management grantor options in their courses in estate planning; Second, states that grant misleading certification of attorneys as specialists in estate planning; Third, attorneys who do not advise grantors of their financial options or where to seek advice on these issues as required by the lawyer's professional code of ethics; Fourth, insurance companies whose coverage wrongfully contributes to the loss of malpractice insurance if an attorney gives financial and investment advice in estate planning.

These factors are what others do not want you to know. Once you are aware of them, it is your responsibility to spend time reviewing your rights before you visit a trust attorney. The rights are easy to understand and are summarized in the check list starting on page 159 .

If you need help, interview a financial planner or a CPA to determine their knowledge and experience to assist you.

Lawyers flood web, many fail to tell whole truth

"For unscrupulous lawyers, the Web is the perfect marketing tool - cheap, pervasive and lacking serious regulation."[1] The Wall Street Journal ran a front-page story on this subject.[1] In it the Journal

(1)   Wall Street Journal, Monday, January 15, 2001 issue.

referred to "suspended attorneys who hang virtual shingles online, foiling ethics watchdogs."

The article gave examples of clever web sites that failed to disclose that the attorney was under suspension. So, remember to be careful of strangers - especially those on Web sites.

<u>False economy in a kit</u>

You can buy estate planning kits on the Web. You can also buy them in stores. The price on the Web runs from a low of about $9.95 to a high of around $ 1,250. Kits at local stores can be under $20.00.

None of these preprinted forms include any of the options we recommend to properly provide for and protect your family. These forms use boilerplate provisions and require the grantors to fill in the blanks for general type questions. They are inexpensive but inadequate.

Your Rights are Missing From Most Estate Plans

Your Constitutional rights

Your rights to your property are clearly stated in our Constitution. These rights apply during a person's life and after their death. It is our property and we control its use.

Depending upon the types of property owned, there are some limitations on the use of it such as real estate zoning laws. But essentially any legal act for the use and control of property continues after the death of the owner, if proper legal documents stating the owner's wishes were prepared.

The only general limitations are that the use of property after a person's death must be for the benefit of the heirs and the use must be lawful.

If we have what politicians consider to be too much wealth, governments may pass laws confiscating part of our estates. But what remains is still ours to control after we die. What most grantors don't realize is that they have given away their rights in the boilerplate provisions found in most estate planning documents.

Determine what you want to do with your estate

The important issue in planning a Trust is determining what you want to accomplish with your estate. This requires decisions that can only be made by you. Many of them concern financial and management aspects of your document. You can place directives in your Trust stating how you want these financial and management issues handled by your trustee. If you do that you will make your Trust an effective document that will properly provide for and protect your family and other heirs.

A check list of your Rights

Before meeting with the attorney who is to prepare your estate plan, the sensible grantor will do some personal preparation. To assist in this, we have prepared a check list of key financial and management options. See page 159.

You should consider this check list carefully. It is the first step in your estate plan. Once you have considered the direction you want to go in, give a copy of this list with your preferences to the attorney you plan to use.

Laws Governing Trusts

You should be aware that the laws governing Trusts are of two types:

1. Laws of the first type deal with tax issues such as how much of your estate you can leave tax free; limitations on the powers of the income beneficiary, and many other tax related issues. These laws are mainly federal government laws. States also have estate-tax laws and most states also tax estates. You cannot change these laws. Your Trust must conform to them. This is an area in which your Trust attorney should be well trained. When he prepares your Trust, he will make continual reference to the

various tax code sections.[1]

2.   Laws of the second   type deal with issues grantors neglected to address in their Trust documents. Each state has laws that address these neglected issues and the laws are called "Default Rules."[2] They control what will happen to the funds in your Trust and hence   the resulting   income to your spouse, the expected end-value of the Trust for your children and many other important issues. You have the authority to override these Default Rules and you should take the opportunity to do so by exercising your options.

If you fail to do so, your Trust is said to be "silent" on any option you did not address The state will then determine how these most important issues will be handled. It is like dying without a Will. You did not make your intentions known when you should have done so.

It is in this second area of Trust law that you should control and use your options. Your Trust attorney should know the Default Rules of your state. But many

---

(1)   There are numerous regulations that Trust attorneys continually study for guidance in Trust work. These include: the Internal Revenue Code; Private Letter Rulings issued by the IRS; Official Rulings of the IRS; Treasury Regulations; and statutes and court rulings of their state. These references to government ruling and laws are listed in just about every section of your documents and make it very hard for the reader to understand what is provided for their family.

(2)   Dictionary definition of default "is a failure to act - neglect." In law, a default is defined as "an omission."

attorneys do not understand how these state rules apply to the financial and management options that you should consider, options recommended in this book.

The reason for this is that attorneys have not been trained in this area. They are not aware of how omitting or including option language will affect the financial outcome. Some don't know if clearly stated Default Rules even exit for some of the options you want.

You must use the services of someone with knowledge of these key financial and management options if you are to get a strong and worthwhile document. Your best bet may be a financial advisor who has been trained in these important estate planning issues.

If a grantor does not take the time to plan what their Trust is to provide, the attorney can only prepare a Trust document that will contain boilerplate provisions controlled by the Default Rules. Your inability to state your intentions means you have no assurance of what will happen with your assets after your death.

You have, in effect, given up your rights to control your property. But you do not have to do that.

Your rights to override the Default Rules.

You have a right to override the Default Rules of the state where you reside. This right is clearly stated in the new "Uniform Prudent Investor Act" (UPIA) currently the law in twenty-three states and being considered for adoption by many others.[3]

SECTION 1. The "Uniform Prudent Investor Act" states:

"(a)   Except as otherwise provided in subsection (b), a trustee who invests and manages assets owes a duty to the beneficiaries of the trust to comply with the prudent investor rule set forth in this [Act]."

"(b)   The prudent investor rule, <u>a default rule,</u> may be expanded, restricted, eliminated or otherwise altered by the provisions of a trust. A trustee is not liable to a beneficiary to the extent that the trustee acted in reasonable reliance on the provisions of the trust."

Carefully read what section 1 (b), above, says. The new law itself is a Default Rule and it is a beneficial one. It states that you have the right (as stated in section 1 (b)) to put into your Trust what you want to have happen with the funds in your Trust - how they will be invested and managed. You personally can better determine such things as the income your surviving spouse will need, and the potential end-value of the Trust for your children and other heirs.

You have the right to expand upon, restrict, eliminate or otherwise alter this law to accommodate your wishes. Your trustee is to act upon these Directives

(3)   See Appendix F for a listing of states that have adopted this UPIA, a copy of it, and comments on key sections.

and is not accountable to a beneficiary of your Trust for following your clearly stated instructions.

Grantors who neglect their rights should be aware that those they care about can be subject to years of misunderstanding, dissent and family unrest. Much of this can be traced to boilerplate generalities that blur the intentions of the Trust.

With all of the good things you can leave your heirs, don't have them inherit bitter feelings, family disharmony and perhaps even hatred.

Do them all a favor, including your trustee. Know your financial and management intentions and express them specifically. It is your right!

In some cases, even where a Default Rule is favorable, you should consider stating your specific instructions anyway. This will help avoid problems that arise, should there be later changes in the Default Rules of your state or the state that may later control your document.

We will show in Chapter 7 the substantial difference in outcome from a $675,000 Credit Shelter Trust. It can provide the annual income a surviving spouse needs (which could be $35,000 a year), instead of the $20,000 she will get before state and federal taxes, when the "Default Rules"prevail. You will also learn about other important financial and management options you have.

A second look at your right under the law

A second look at your rights under the law can be found in Federal Regulations of National banks. National banks are supervised by the Comptroller of the Currency, a federal office.

Under Federal Law:

"The Fiduciary (your trustee) must manage investments in accordance with the terms of the governing instrument,[4] which is the primary determinant of a fiduciary's powers and duties. If the instrument is silent as to authorized investments, the trustee is guided by provisions of local law."

From: Page 49, "Comptroller's Handbook for Fiduciary Activities," Comptroller of the Currency, Administrator of National Banks. Code of Federal Regulations regarding trusts.

The statement above is another example of your rights to override the Default Rules of your state government and the Default Rules of any other state government. This is one of the many reasons why you can place the provision in your Trust that will allow you, or others after your death, to change the state that controls the Trust by simply filing a letter with the Trust indicating the change.

If used, your rights are very powerful

We will show you examples of how strong your rights are under the law. You can state in your Trust

(4)   The "governing instrument" is your Trust document.

how you want your assets invested. So powerful are your rights that if you stated that 100% of your assets must be held in cash, the courts in all likelihood would not change your directive. They may agree to a petition to at least hold the cash in insured savings accounts in order to obtain a small amount of interest.

THE COURTS HAVE RULED . . . .

IF YOU WANT SOMETHING TO HAPPEN - PUT IT IN YOUR TRUST - OTHERWISE THE "DEFAULT RULES" WILL CONTROL THE ACTIONS OF YOUR TRUSTEE.

Even in instances that seem not entirely sensible, the courts are very reluctant to issue a ruling to change directives stated in a Trust. This is noted in the court ruling below:

"Except where impossible, illegal, or where a change of circumstances occurs which would impair the purposes of the Trust, the nature and extent of the duties and powers of a trustee are determined by the Trust instrument."[3]

In Chapter 7 we will present differences in the income needs of a surviving husband and a surviving wife. In most Trusts, they both will receive the same low annual income no matter who the surviving spouse is. Why?

This occurs because with the exception of the differences in their names, the Trusts of most husbands and the Trusts of their wives read exactly the same. And, why is this?

If you and your spouse already have Credit Shelter Trusts, compare one to the other. Place them side by side and on a separate page write the name of each article in the Trusts. Note any difference in the sections between the husband's Trust and the wife's Trust.

You will find, as have many, that the provisions of both husband's and wife's are basically the same and neither document addresses their different economic needs. This is a failing. Economic needs are rarely the same for every individual. As an example, many husbands have pensions, that continue when their wives die. But if the husband dies first, as happens in four out of five marriages, the wife may receive only

(3)   Allen v. Pacific National Bank 99 Wash.2d 394, 633 P.2nd 104

half or none of the husband's pension. Therefore her income is immediately curtailed. Her needs are a lot different financially than her husband's. But the Trust does not recognize this key estate-planning fact.

In addition, the Trusts with such problems that we reviewed contained no instructions to solve these problems or override the Default Rules. This strongly suggests that in each case, the grantor was not aware that these Rules would govern the Trust. No power to override Default Rules weakens a Trust and seriously impacts financial benefits to the heirs.

Keep in mind that a Trust is a contract . You have rights to clearly state what you want to have happen with the assets in your estate. Contracts cannot be restricted by the laws of any state.[4] This is an important reason to include a provision in your Trust that allows you (or others after your death) to change the state that controls it. You do this by filing a letter with the Trust document stating the transfer of the Trust to the control of another state.

In this book, we will explain each of your major financial options and their resulting economic benefits. They are summarized in a check list starting on page 159

---

(4)   Clause 1 of Section 10 of the United States Constitution applies to trust contracts. Clause 1 states: No State shall pass any law impairing the obligation of contracts.

Chapter 3

Determine What You Want to Accomplish

Plan what you want before you visit an attorney

Before you visit a Trust attorney, you need to determine what you want to financially accomplish with your estate after your death. You also need to be aware of some management issues that you need to consider. This work is not hard to do. The starting point for most Trusts, the income of the surviving spouse, is discussed in Chapter 7.

You also have the option of increasing the end-value of your Trust for your children and other heirs (see Chapter 10). If you have only one child, who will inherit your entire estate, you may (or may not) consider their inheritance of up to $2 million or more, tax free, as a substantial enough sum for this one child to receive.

If you have several children plus grandchildren, you may want to consider giving investment instructions in your estate plan to obtain a potentially greater end-value of your Trust since it will be divided among so many.

REMEMBER:

YOU HAVE THE RIGHT TO STATE WHAT YOU WANT TO HAVE HAPPEN WITH THE FAMILY ASSETS YOU PLACE IN YOUR TRUST

YOU HAVE THE RIGHT TO:

1. DETERMINE the annual income your

surviving spouse is to receive from the Trust.

2.   STATE how the funds are to be invested.

3.   PROVIDE for a higher end-value of the
     Trust for the benefit of your children,
     grandchildren and other heirs.

4.   PROVIDE safeguards for the assets in your
     Trust for the protection of your family.

5.   PROVIDE other important financial and
     management options available to you for
     inclusion in your Trust.

If you first consult standard Trust forms sold in stationery stores or over the Internet, they will probably not give you a document that will provide a satisfactory Trust for the needs of your family. The advice and considerations you need go beyond what standard forms provide.

Some books on Trusts also provide standard forms. Are your key options in these forms? How could they be unless the needs of your family are the same as everyone else's family goals and objectives. If you doubt this, compare these standard forms to the options in this book. [1]

(1) It may be difficult, at first, to understand the legal wording
       of any Trust you review to determine what options are in that
       Trust. One quick test is to look for the income the person
       named in the Trust is to receive. If the Trust reads "My
       Trustee is to pay my surviving spouse the net income from the
       trust" then a boilerplate provision was used and your spouse
       may only receive half the income needed.

Some banks may recommend Trust attorneys to help you. Banks have traditionally been the professional managers of Trusts. Their marketing efforts, in the past, have been strongly tied to attorney referrals. Their referrals are often to attorneys that the bank has worked with in the past and with whom they do business. They may be good, but the referral alone is no guarantee that these are the best Trust attorneys in your area.

<u>An attorney can only give you a boilerplate Trust if you can not state what you want.</u>

Most Trust attorneys state that each Trust they prepare is tailored to individual needs. But, if the grantors do not clearly state their objectives, the attorneys are limited in what they can provide beyond the legal issues relating to the tax code,

There are some Trust attorneys who will advise you of your Trust options as outlined in this book. Attorneys who do this generally have available to them one or more persons, trained in many of these financial options, who will work with you as part of a team to prepare your Trust. Very wealthy people want this type of estate planning and are prepared to pay for it. The fee they pay for this service is generally over $15,000.

If your estate is under $ 4 or 5 million , you can obtain the same basic benefits for your family by considering the financial options in this book.

<u>Beware of an attorney recommended by a friend</u>

A friend who has established a Trust may

recommend the attorney who has prepared his, confident that he has a Trust that will properly provide for his family. Such recommendations are often based on the fact that the Trust was prepared at a reasonable cost or that the preparer was a "nice person." A good Trust document that will adequately protect and provide for your family and has been prepared based on your needs is expensive - but worth the cost. You can substantially reduce this expense by giving your attorney examples of what you want.

A review of your friend's Trust more than likely would reveal that it does not contain the options presented in this book. If these options are missing, your friend's Trust will be governed by Default Rules. These rules may impact the financial course of a Trust in a way not envisioned or understood by your friend or by most grantors. Protecting and providing for the family is one of the main objectives of a Trust and that is the financial course on which the grantor should focus.

You and every grantor can plan for and provide for most of the important issues relating to your financial plan. You can make appropriate directives in your Trust. Do not make the mistake of relying on the Default Rules, or presuming you have no options.

As an example, if your wife is the surviving spouse and later in her life she is confined to a nursing home, would you want your children to visit her? Bring the grandchildren? Determine if she is being properly cared for? This would normally be done if the children lived nearby, but if they live at great distances, you can provide for the expense of these visits in your Trust

Brokerage firms want your business but cannot help you prepare your estate plan.

Most brokerage firms want your Trust business. All of the larger firms have established Trust operations. But the sales people in many of these firms do not understand the options you have and would want in your Trust. Few can help you determine the income requirements for your surviving spouse or advise you that directives must be placed in a Trust to increase the value of it for your children.

All corporations look at their market opportunities coupled with their resources and capabilities. Once this has been determined, they set about to organize their company to capture these market opportunities. But this has not happened in the brokerage industry.

Instead, the brokerage industry has hired trust attorneys and former bank trust officers, people who do not necessarily understand a grantor's financial and management options. They are trained to provide boilerplate forms. As a result they restrict their firm's market opportunities to about 10% of the Trust business that uses professional trustees to manage Trust money. They have ignored the other 90% which they are in a strong position to attract. They can do this by using their firm's resource of a large and financially trained sales force. It seems a natural role for them to explain to clients and prospects these financial and management options as grantor has.

Independent financial advisors do understand this market opportunity and can be the best source of assistance.

Banks are not willing to help you

Banks, like brokerage houses, should be able to help you. But the trust departments of banks, like brokerage houses, are controlled by attorneys, not business people.

Attorneys know they are not allowed, in this country, to provide legal services to the customers of their banks or their brokerage firms.

But this restriction on attorneys not to preform legal services when employed by corporations has gone too far.

There is a major distinction between providing *legal services* (such as writing Wills and Trusts) and providing *legal information*. The attorneys employed by banks and brokerage firms should be willing to provide legal information to clients and prospects and assist in training the sales people of the banks to provide the type of information that is included in this book. Financial guidance at the trust department of a bank or a brokerage firm should be available to their clients and prospects. In less than five years from now, the financial advisors employed by brokerage firms will be giving this financial advice. Banks will probably maintain their hands off attitude and are expected to experience a decline in future trust business.

People need advice on financial and management options and anyone can give it

Anyone can give legal advice. The president of

the American Bar Association has clearly stated this fact. And, has stated also that only attorneys can provide legal services. This distinction needs to be understood.

Anyone can tell you the expected financial results from a contract (which is what a Trust is). And anyone can advise you about financial and management considerations to be placed in a legal document that an attorney will prepare.

Some Certified Public Accounting organizations do not understand this. I am aware of one executive director of a state CPA organization who continually cautions the state's CPAs that they will lose their state license as a CPA if they ever discuss legal issues or even have a law book in their office. This executive director is an attorney. Who do you think he represents with this misleading advice- the CPAs who pay his salary or the legal profession that he belongs to?

In estate planning, the legal profession has much to be ashamed of and much to correct

Some in the legal profession will claim that a person who gives financial and management advice on issues to be considered in a contract is practicing law without a license. This is pure nonsense and wrongfully propagated by a few people in that profession.

Some state bar associations are still attempting to enforce restrictions on anyone, other than a lawyer, who gives advice on financial and management issues that are missing from or should be considered in legal documents.

As mentioned in Chapter 1, in the area of estate planning (granting certifications to attorneys that appear similar in stature to those given in the medical profession) is the fault of state supreme courts. They yield to pressure from bar associations.

It is a deceptive practice for a state supreme court to convey "Board Certified Specialist in Estate Planning" when those so certified have no knowledge of, are not tested on, nor required to have demonstrated their knowledge of the vital options a grantor has to protect and provide for their family.

This practice by courts, such as the Supreme Court of South Carolina, gives credence to the worst meaning of the phrase - "it is a court of law not of justice." It is the culmination of complete disrespect by the legal profession for the general public. These actions make no sense and benefit none but a few attorneys attempting to charge high fees, and have only resulted in disrespect for the legal profession. With a little thought and consideration of the citizens of their state, the courts could have developed and required standards for an estate planning speciality that would be of great benefit to both the citizens of their state and to the lawyers who practice there.

But South Carolina, and a few other states, have been satisfied to pass off a questionable certification on to many unsuspecting people.

We are a country of laws. But not of the type of laws that clearly foster a medieval guild mentality. But this is an attitude, undoubtably prompted by greed, of a few estate planning attorneys. It has been carelessly endorsed by state bars, state courts, and is a mentality that has gained acceptance by the legal profession.

The personal and professional limitations of those who should be able to assist you, should not prevent you from getting the help you need from a different source.

If you need help, who can you turn to?

If you need help, your best starting point is with a financial planner trained in grantor's financial and management options in estate planning. A good estate planning attorney may be able to recommend such a person.

If the financial planner is registered as an investment advisor, he or she will be required to give you a copy of his or her current Form ADV as required by the S. E. C. [2]

If you want an effective and specific estate planning document do not be fooled by the old and incorrect statement: "You cannot anticipate everything and therefore you should let the trustee make those decisions if and when these things come up." In other words, don't bother including what you want covered.

An example is a couple who lived on the East Coast and had two daughters. Each daughter was

---

(2)   Copies of a persons Form ADV that will disclose information about their education, practice, compensation and fees can be obtained directly from the SEC (Securities Exchange Commission) by calling their Headquarters in Washington, D.C.

THESE EXPERTS CAN ASSIST YOU.
BUT YOU ARE THE ONLY EXPERT
ON THE NEEDS OF YOUR FAMILY

married with children. One daughter lived in the Los
Angeles area, the other in Denver. Their husbands
worked but they were not wealthy.

Every other year the parents paid the airfare for
their   daughters,   their   husbands   and   their
grandchildren to visit them for a week. They rented a
seaside house for their visitors, near their own home,
and spent part of each day with them.

However, if one of the parents passed away,
such visits would probably not continue. Their Trusts
had no provision to pay the expenses of family visits. In
fact, there was no provision to pay for any travel
expense of their daughters to visit the surviving spouse,
even if that person was ill or in a nursing home . Funds
were available in their Trusts, but access to them for
this purpose was not provided. We do not know of any
state's Default Rule that would require the trustee to
pay the travel and other related expenses for these
visits, even if the surviving spouse was ill or in a
nursing home. Consideration for including this type of
expenditure in a Trust is very important

You the grantor can require the trustee to pay
travel and other expenses associated with family visits
if you clearly state so in the Trust documentation. A
trustee handles the investments, but family members
have a greater interest in determining if the surviving
spouse is receiving proper care and attention in a
nursing home or, if a change to another facility is
required. The joy such visits can bring to the surviving
parent will not be found in the "Default Rules."

This family that lived many miles apart, was able

to do this because an attorney later inserted authorization into the parent's Trusts, for travel and lodging payments for their daughters' families. It made it possible for them to visit whether the surviving parent was in good health, ill or in a nursing facility.

When you review the material in this book, note the reasons for using each option presented. You will also find them summarized in the check list starting on page 159. The material offers important financial considerations and other options that may be in the best interests of the surviving spouse and the family.

What you must do

Before you visit a Trust attorney, you must determine what you want to accomplish with your estate after your death. It is a revealing and rewarding process that only you can do.

If you are uncertain about what to expect in the way of services from a Trust attorney - think back on an early experience, that of buying your first home. You told the attorney the location of the house, the price you would pay for it, a mortgage and interest charges, and whether any items of personal property were to be part of the purchase (appliances, window treatments, etc.).

This is the decision work you do whether you are buying a home or starting a business and it is important that you do it when you establish your Trust. You first determine what you want to accomplish.

A.   You must determine the income needs of yourself, your surviving spouse, and other income beneficiaries from the Trust. Use Exhibits 1 & 2 shown in Chapter 7 with instructions in Appendix G.

B.   You must determine the desired end-value of the Trust for your children (see Chapter 10) and many other key financial and management options they have and can place in their Trusts.

C.   You must determine how best to provide for the spouse of a second marriage and your own children (see Chapter 12).

D.   You must determine the safeguards you want in your Trust and the other options presented in this book and that are available to you.

E.   You must determine a very important but rarely stated objective: how to maintain a strong family relationship between and among the surviving spouse and the children.

Saving Estate Taxes

Avoiding federal estate taxes

Avoiding and reducing federal estate taxes have been two driving forces in many estate plans. Married couples have been able to combine their individual federal estate-tax exemptions to double the amount of money they can leave tax free to their children and other heirs. Other types of Trusts have been developed to reduce the value of a person's assets at their death and these are discussed in Chapter 18.

What changes will be required in existing estate plans based on changes in federal estate taxes? Should married couples continue to hold assets in separate names if there will be no federal estate tax on their assets?

The first thing to be aware of is that the new federal tax code may only be a temporary situation. Later administrations can reverse any estate-tax relief and create new taxes on estates. High taxation of the wealthy is the trend in our government. Future. Presidents and a Congress, with additional socialistic thinking representatives, can reverse any estate-tax relief and create new taxes on estates. So adoption of President Bush's estate-tax relief should be viewed as a temporary measure. To benefit from the new federal estate-tax code, transfers of assets should be made in such a way as to be "grandfathered"[1] from being

(1)   In most instances transactions completed prior to the date of a new law affecting these types of transactions are exempted from the new law. However, there cannot be any guarantee that this will happen.

included in any new taxation on estates and wealth.

There will be many ways proposed to avoid future taxation of estates. But many of these plans will severely limit the control the current owners will have over their property that is placed in irrevocable Trusts.

You need to avoid state and local taxes

State and local governments depend upon estate taxes as part of their needed annual income. And they will increase their estate taxes as federal estate taxes are reduced. These new and additional taxes on estates will be a source of much needed income for states and local governments who levy them.

For most people, estate planning documents must contain directives that will provide for the avoidance of these state and local taxes of estates and trusts.

The net result of the new federal estate-tax code will be an increase in the amount of estate taxes collected by the individual states, The amount of additional estate taxes will continue to vary state by state. But in general the total amount of estate taxes collected by the states will be increasing. The true result of President's Bush's reductions in federal estate taxes will be that a major part of the federal decrease in estate- tax income will become a source of additional estate-tax income for the states.

When the new federal estate-tax reductions are phased in and become law, there is no requirement that state tax exemptions be the same as the federal.

that state tax exemptions be the same as the federal.

It means estate taxes will not be eliminated at the state and local government level. In fact, taxes will be increased since there will be available to the states more assets to tax as federal estate taxes are eliminated.

An example of this can be seen in the federal and state tax amounts for an estate worth $1,675,000 in 2000. This estate is $1 million over the federal estate tax exemption in 2000. Using North Carolina as a typical state, the taxes on this $1 million over the federal estate -tax exemption was:

Federal estate taxes	$345,800
North Carolina estate taxes	33,200
Total Estate Taxes	$379,000

With the elimination of federal estate taxes on the above $1 million, North Carolina and other states would have an opportunity to double or triple their tax on estates. And many states like North Carolina have financial problems and need sources of funds.

The trick for the wise will be to have your Trust capable of being moved from a high tax state to a low tax state. And, this capability can work not only to reduce the estate taxes due at death but also to reduce the annual taxes on the estates (Trusts) after the grantor's death.

<u>Wording to avoid state and local taxes</u>

All major estate planning documents should have

a separate article that allows you to change the state that controls your Trust. This is accomplished by simply filing a letter with the document stating that the Trust is now controlled by the new state you name and designate.

Including this separate article in your document will have important advantages during your lifetime and after your death.

The first thing it does is allow you to move to another state without the expense of rewriting your Trust. After your death, the Trust is not locked-in forever to the laws and annual taxes of that state. This is an important option should later laws prove disadvantageous.

This option should be included when you establish a Living Trust and is sufficient reason to revise existing Trusts. The same recommendation for using this option would apply to other types of Trusts, some of which are irrevocable, such as a Charitable Remainder Trust. Trusts always contain references to the statutes of a state whose Default Rules cover many Trust issues. Some of those state laws either now or in the future may have disadvantages for your heirs. For this reason you always want to be able to change the state of jurisdiction that controls your Trust.

<u>Wording to put into your Trust</u>

•   Your current residence generally determines the state that controls your Trust. At some later date you may want to move out of the state and you should be able to direct that this new state of residence will control your Trust. This is done by an instrument, such as a letter signed by you as trustee of your Living Trust, and filed with the Trust records. You can do this to avoid having a new Trust prepared.

- Another reason for your Trust to have this change may be for your own tax benefits, for your heirs or for any reason you deem appropriate. You as trustee of your Living Trust should have this authority to move your Trust to another state. It is possible after your death, that your surviving spouse may move to another state or a successor trustee may already be in another state. You want your heirs and trustee to have the option to change the jurisdiction of your Trust if it is of benefit to do so.

- Changing the state of jurisdiction is done by putting into your document the ability to do so. It will apply to any part of the property in the Trust, including real estate. States do not like to release control of real estate in their jurisdiction. But they may be forced to do so if the above option, properly worded by your attorney, is included in your Trust.

I am indebted to Alex Webb, an attorney and CPA practicing in Aberdeen and Wilmington, North Carolina, for permission to use his material on this important option that follows:

Construction

"The terms and provisions of this Agreement (TRUST) shall be construed, regulated and governed as to administration and as to validity and effect by the laws of the State of *(Name of State)*. To minimize any tax in respect to this trust, or any beneficiary thereof, or for such other purpose as it deems appropriate, the Trustee may in its sole and absolute discretion remove all or any part of the property of or the situs of administration of, such trust from one jurisdiction to another and elect, by an instrument filed with the trust records, that thereafter such trust shall be construed, regulated and governed as to administration by the laws of such other jurisdiction. Furthermore, if the trustee is changed to a trustee in another jurisdiction, then in the instrument of appointment, the applicable law may be changed to such new jurisdiction or remain the law of *(Name of State)* as the parties thereto elect."

After your death, your surviving spouse or other income beneficiary may want to move from the current state to a state that incidentally has lower annual estate taxes on the assets and income of the Trust.

And, it is also possible to transfer the Trust to a state that has little or no estate taxes at the death of the grantor and no annual taxes on the income and value of the Trust.

Delaware and others too, have always been looking for ways to attract corporations and assets. It benefits the professionals of these states, especially attorneys and bankers. And, the state also benefits from increased taxes paid by these professionals and their support personnel.

Estates Under $ 750,000

<u>Special needs of your Family</u>

Some generalizations can be made about what should be considered when planning estate documents. But of greater importance are the special family circumstances and the specific needs of individuals in those families and all can vary greatly. When estate plans are made for those with assets under $750,000, they are not made to save federal estate taxes. There are no federal estate taxes on estates under this amount. And, in 2006 there will be no federal estate taxes on estates under $ 1 million.

When the estate is under $750,000 the plan is made because a particular need is recognized such as providing an income and support for someone who may be too young to manage their inheritance or simply not able to do so. A plan for an estate in this category may have the grantor provide an income for someone, such as a spouse in a second marriage, but still control who will receive the funds after that spouse's death. Avoiding the costs and time delays of probate is also a very good reason for having a Living Trust prepared..

<u>Avoiding probate</u>

The assets in your estate should be placed in a position to avoid probate. The costs of probate can be 2 to 4% or more of your estate and take six months or longer. Probate requires advertizing your death and reference that your Will and a listing of your assets and copies of it be available for anyone who is interested in having them. These added costs, the delays, and arranging for the public to be informed of your assets, their values, the terms and conditions in your Will and all who are to receive them, can be avoided.

If you are a single person

If you are a single person, you will need to consider a Living Trust to avoid probate. It allows you to name many beneficiaries, retain complete control of the assets you place in this Living Trust, remove or add assets to it and change your beneficiaries as many times as you wish along with the amount and the terms and conditions each will receive as their legacy.

Transfer-on-death or joint accounts

You can also consider a Transfer-On Death(TOD) account or a Payable-On- Death (POD) account or for assets that can held in a bank or at a brokerage firm. These accounts avoid probate. You retain control of the account while alive, but at your death the assets avoid probate and pass directly to your named beneficiary.

These types of accounts are safer than establishing a joint account with a beneficiary. A co-owner (other than yourself) of a joint account has the right to use all of the money in the account without your permission. The creditors of a person who is listed on the joint account can also obtain funds in the account.

TOD or POD accounts have advantages over joint accounts. They are very easy to set up. The other person named cannot get at the assets nor can their creditors while you are alive.   If your state has not yet established these types of accounts, you can set them up

with a bank or brokerage firm located in one of the
many other states that has passed TOD or POD laws.

<u>If you are married</u>

If you are married, you can have the assets
placed in the names of each individual partner with the
title passing to the survivor at the death of either party.
This will avoid probate - but only at the death of the
first party. It would be a better plan to establish now a
Living Trust for both of you while you are still alive and
heathy. This will permit each spouse's estate to avoid
probate.

There are other benefits too. If a surviving spouse
is incapable of managing affairs, family members or
other persons could be named to serve as successor
trustees, thus avoiding delays and legal costs.

If married, you may have the title to your
assets in both names with "right of survivorship." This
too avoids probate upon the death of the first individual.
Title to your bank accounts, stocks and bonds,
brokerage accounts[1] and most other items held in your

1)   A simple method to change title to securities held in one
      person's name is to open a brokerage account and deposit
      the securities in this new account. After you receive your
      first monthly statement, ask the broker to change title to
      include your spouse with "right of survivorship." If later
      you again want to hold your securities, instruct your broker
      to register and ship the   securities to you. When the
      securities arrive they should be in joint names with the
      wording "right of survivorship" clearly stated. This
      procedure should also be used if you are changing the titles
      of the securities from your name (or the names of you and
      your spouse) to the name of your Living Trust.

name can and should be changed to joint accounts with "right of survivorship" or at least to a TOD (Transfer-On Death) or POD (Payable-On-Death) accounts.

<u>Check the title to your home</u>

Be careful of how the title of assets in real estate read. For many married couples their home is their largest single asset. And, while they know that their home is listed in both of their names, they do not know if the listing reads "with right of survivorship" or as "tenancy in common." Many years may have passed since a married couple purchased their home. Few individuals I have talked with could remember, for certain, what the title actually said. A quick check of court house records will provide the answer. Do not overlook this very important issue.

In many states the general practice is to place the titles in each person's name as "tenancy in common."

This means that there is no right of survivorship. The deceased person's share passes to their estate. The home and any other real estate that is jointly owned goes to the probate court to change the title upon the death of the first owner. The probate expense can be many thousands of dollars in addition to the time delays. The property cannot be sold or mortgaged until this title problem is corrected.

For about $75.00 you can change the title of your home from "tenancy in common" to "right of survivorship." I recommend that everyone obtain from court records the knowledge of how their property is jointly titled. The later expenses are too great if the title is not correct for your estate plan.[2]

<u>Special circumstances to consider</u>

This is the most important item to be considered for most of us. Can I leave the assets directly to those individuals that I want to have them? For most married people with assets under $ 750,000 this is the correct thing to do. Leave what you have directly to your spouse. If you established a Living Trust, make sure your surviving spouse will have an adequate annual income (see Chapter 7) and give serious consideration to providing your spouse with control of the items in our check list, starting on page 159 Upon the surviving spouse's death, the assets remaining in the Living Trust go to your children and other heirs per your instructions.

The directives you can place in your Living Trust can change the terms and conditions of how your assets are given.

After the death of the first spouse, the surviving spouse is of course, a single person. That surviving spouse, now a single person, cannot use joint accounts to escape probate. But answers can be found to this. Review prior pages on the advantages of TOD or POD accounts.

Unless the surviving spouse has a Living Trust, most assets must pass through probate upon their death. So, if the surviving spouse must consider a Living

(2)   For some married people, with assets over $ 750,000, it may be best to have title to their home or other property as "tenancy in common." Which type of title is best to use depends upon how their assets will be divided to fund their Living Trust.

Trust, why not do it immediately. This is another reason why we recommend that the assets be placed now in a Living Trust while both partners are alive vs. later in life when the surviving partner may forget to do so or be mentally incapacitated.

For most married couples, having a Living Trust prepared while each is alive is generally the best consideration.

<u>Other key considerations</u>

There are other issues and documents to be considered and these should be put in place while you are still young and in good health. Items like power of attorney, medical care directives, living wills, etc. should be prepared and signed (see Chapter 17). The existence and location of these documents should be known. Much grief and concern can result if the documents are not available. And remember, you can always change these documents if that is your wish.

Estates Over $ 750,000

Estate taxes should not control your planning

Once estates exceed $ 750,000 and have assets that are expected to increase in value, Wills and Trusts are prepared by most people. Unfortunately, what we read and hear is the need to escape estate taxes. While this is an important consideration, it should only be pursued after first planning for the needs and the protection of the family.

Needs of your family come first

When you are thinking of having a Will or a Trust prepared, you should plan what you want to accomplish for your family. Their needs must be planned by you before obtaining the assistance of a Trust attorney.

Unfortunately, many grantors believe that they have few options in their estate plans, that state and federal laws control their estates, that estate planning documents (Wills and Trusts) are standard forms. As a result of these incorrect beliefs many grantors seek an attorney who will prepare their documents for a low fixed fee. These documents are much too important to be dismissed without serious consideration.

In a recent survey[1] attorneys were asked their opinion on the following statements:

"Under the misconception that the law allows few options in Trusts, people look for an attorney who will prepare their documents for the lowest fixed fee."

(1)   Survey sent to 4,250 attorneys

- 73% of the attorneys who responded agreed with the above statement - 17% had no opinion; 5% disagreed and 5% did not answer.

When the attorneys were asked about the following statement:

"A Trust can be tailored to the needs of a person's individual family"

-95% of the attorneys who responded agreed with the above statement - 5% had no opinion.

And when the attorneys were asked:

"To obtain the annual income a surviving spouse may need from a Trust may require overriding the Default Rules of the state.

- 70% of the attorneys who responded agreed with the above statement - 22% had no opinion;[2] 3% disagreed and 5% did not answer.

To have a proper Trust prepared it must be tailored to the needs of your family and your wishes as the grantor. It will cost more than a standard form document. But the added legal expense is minor compared to the benefits your family will receive.

2)   Approximately 2,500 of the attorneys in the survey did not specialize in estate planning but listed their work as a general practice. Therefore, many may not have been aware of the provisions of the state Default Rules on Income when a Trust was silent as to the specific payments.

Boilerplate in your documents? - a quick test

A quick test to determine if boilerplate provisions are in your Trust is to look for the instructions to the trustee on income payments to your spouse. Does the Trust have the following directive?

> *"My Trustee shall pay my surviving spouse the net income from the Trust."*

Wife receives half of income needed

If the above phrase is in your Will or Trust, then the wife, as the surviving spouse will receive a very low income. This boilerplate phrase provides an income, before state and federal income taxes, that can be less than 3% of the value of assets.

For most wives this will only provide about half the income they need and could have received if proper attention had been paid to their needs.

How to determine the income needs of each spouse is presented in the next chapter.

Check list for family needs

For a summary of your rights and family needs see the check list on page 159. Have copies made and give these requirements to your estate planning attorney.

High value estate considerations

A high value estate is one whose assets exceed

the living needs of the individual and their spouse. People with estates of this type need to start now to give funds away. This is done not only to reduce the value of the estate but also to assist in the transfer of wealth to children and other heirs.

Using the right to make tax-free gifts should be considered. Establishing a gift Trust for children or grandchildren can be a wonderful way to provide for these young people. It can avoid all of the problems with gifts made to a minor under the "UTMA" (Uniform Transfers to Minors Act). Under the "UTMA" children receive these funds when they are 18. Many times they never go to college, use the funds for cars, etc. A gift Trust can avoid this. Funds maybe withheld until age thirty or older but their college expenses can be paid.

A gift Trust can be established for the benefit of one child or several children. If the children are young, the funds in the Trust can grow for ten or more years before any use of these funds maybe required. Part of the lifetime estate tax exemption can be used to place several hundreds of thousands of dollars in this type of Trust. Grandparents, parents and other family members can each contribute up to $10,000 a year to each of these special Trusts.

The grantor can instruct the trustee to pay for educational needs and to provide funds for other worthwhile activities. The time the children must receive any of the income and principal can be delayed until they are mature and have demonstrated their ability to manage money. Additional information on special trusts and additional methods to reduce estate taxes are in Chapter 18.

Planned Income Trust
(or be prepared to live on a lot less)

You must pick the needed income

This chapter presents the information you will need to give financial directives in your Trust to provide the income required for you or your spouse. This is important since over 95% of the Trusts reviewed did not provide an adequate income for the surviving spouse's needs. In fact the shortage can be $10,000 to $20,000 a year. This additional needed income could have been paid from the Trust if proper instructions had been given in the document. This chapter will show how to determine and state the income needed by each person. It is based on common-sense decisions and prudent financial judgment.

When planning a Trust, the most important issue you must determine is the annual income you, your surviving spouse or your other Income Beneficiaries will require, and should receive from the Trust.

This is the starting point - the income to be paid. It is, unfortunately, ignored in most Trusts. Why? Because grantors incorrectly believe that the income to be paid is controlled by Trust law and that they have no rights in this most critical issue. They do not realize that they have an option. As a grantor, you should be very aware of this.

Very few Trust attorneys will assist you in doing the work of personal Trust preparation since they have never been trained in these items. But if you are fortunate enough to have a Trust attorney who will guide you in determining the income needs of each spouse, and other key financial options, the additional legal expense will be minor compared to the benefits you will receive.

<u>Easy form to use</u>

Exhibit 1 and Exhibit 2, on pages 52,and 53 are examples of completed forms to determine the "Income Needs of Each Spouse." In these exhibits the needs of both a husband and the wife[1] are shown on the same form to illustrate that in most cases the wife, as the surviving spouse needs a higher annual income from the Trust.

As you review Exhibit 1, note that the wife will receive a lower Social Security income. Instructions to determine the actual amounts each will receive are in Appendix G. Also note that in this example, if the husband dies first, the wife will only receive 50% of her husband's pension.

The expense items listed in Exhibit 2 for the husband and the wife are the same. The result, at the bottom of Exhibit 2, is that the wife needs a higher income - $18,000 more than the husband's.

Blank copies of Exhibits 1 and 2 are in the back of the book. Make several copies of each form and follow the instructions in Appendix G. Separate forms should be prepared for the husband and the wife. This

(1)   This data is a summary of the class exercise of Trust attorneys attending the author's six-hour CLE (Continuing Legal Education) seminar over the last nine years.

is very important since the sources of income in Exhibit 1 will be different for each surviving spouse. Exhibit 2 is also generally different for each spouse.

You must decide and clearly state in your Trust that this amount is in today's dollars and requires that it be increased each year for inflation and perhaps other considerations. If you do not do this, the income you or your surviving spouse will receive many years later from the Trust can be much lower than needed as a result of inflation. In some cases, the income is disastrously low and different enough from the current life style to cause shock waves.

If you do not do this, the Default Rules of the state will govern the income to be paid. As a general rule when a person does not use their option to give directives *on the amount of income to be paid,* the Default rules provide an income of a little less than 3% of the value of the trust.[2]

Knowing that you must clearly state the income to be received by each spouse is the most important lesson to learn from this book. If you follow only the advice given in this section you will have accomplished a major change in your Trust that can benefit your surviving spouse and your children.

When first completing these forms, it is better to estimate a higher financial need. If after the form is

[2] Because this amount is so low, a few states have recently passed laws stating that at least 4% of the value of the Trust must be paid, if requested.

Exhibit 1
INCOME NEEDS OF EACH SPOUSE

	For John	For Mary
A. ANNUAL INCOME NEEDED before Income Taxes Excluding the cost of a new car and other items listed below	$ 60,000	$ 60,000
B. SOURCES OF INCOME excluding Trust:		
a. Social Security	$ 12,000	$ 9,000
b. Pensions	$ 30,000	$ 15,000
c. IRAs, 401k, etc	$ 5,000	$ 5,000
Sub total	$ 47,000	$ 29,000

B.- d. Other: List by type,

	Current Value	Income	
- Stocks & Mutual Funds	$585,000	$ 11,500	$ 11,500
- Bonds	$100,000	5,500	5,500
- CDs & Saving Account	$100,000	5,000	5,000
Sub Totals	$785,000	$ 22,000	$ 22,000

B. TOTAL SOURCES OF INCOME	$ 69,000	$51,000

PRIOR TO ADDITIONAL SPECIAL NEEDS, SUCH AS:
- Provision for replacement car
- Major home maintenance & Replacement of appliances
- Gifts & assistance to Children
- Travel & Vacations

Status of Income Prior to Special Needs:

- **Husband, John - income surplus of**	$ 9,000	
- **Wife, Mary - income shortage of**		$ 9,000

Exhibit 2   53

INCOME NEEDS OF EACH SPOUSE
FROM THE TRUST

	For John	For Mary
C. Estimated Annual Expenses **For special needs:**		
C-1 Replacement Car costing $20,000 divided by 4 years =	$ 5,000	$ 5,000
C-2 Provision for Major home maintenance & Replacement of appliances	$ 2,500	$ 2,500
C-3 Gifts & assistance to Children and grandchildren	$ 5,000	$ 5,000
C-4 Travel & Vacations	$ 4,000	$ 4,000
C-5 Other Special Needs - List		
C-6 AFTER TAX TOTAL	$ 16,500	$ 16,500

Convert After Tax Total needed for special
needs to an amount prior to federal and state
income taxes: If your top tax bracket is 20%,
increase by 25%; if your top tax bracket is
25%, increase by 33%; if your top tax bracket
is 30%, increase by 43%; if your top tax
bracket is 37% increase by 59%.

	For John	For Mary
INCREASE 43% =	$ 7,095	$ 7,095
D. PRE-TAX TOTAL of Special Needs	$ 23,595	$ 23,595

E. FROM EXHIBIT 1:
Shortage (+) or Surplus (-) of income
Prior to Special Needs   (-)$ 9,000 (+) $ 9,000

F. TOTAL ANNUAL INCOME
REQUIRED FROM TRUST IN
YEAR IT IS EXECUTED (D.+E.) $ 14,595 $ 32,595

*NOTE: The income needs of a widow often exceed those
of a widower, a difference ignored in most documents.*

completed, and the amount of income required from the Trust appears too high, you can always review certain items and reduce them if needed. An estimate on the low side will not provide for the surviving spouse.

NOTE: The surviving spouse should have ample funds available. And, if possible there should be sufficient funds to buy gifts and pay for certain activities for the children and grandchildren. The goal is to maintain a strong family relationship unaffected by financial strain.

Now that you have an understanding of how the Income Needs of Each Spouse was prepared in Exhibit 1, and that these income needs are generally different, you also need to become aware of the following Default Rule regarding how funds are traditionally invested and the resulting income that is paid.

Default Rules control your investments

If you do not say precisely how the assets you place in your Trust are to be invested, the state Default Rules determine how these assets are to be invested.

Many grantors do not understand how investments are to be made based on the following statement that they read in their documents:

"My trustee may invest in stocks, bonds, mutual funds and other types of investments suitable for a trust."

The above is considered a general directive. It excludes stating what percentage of the Trust should be invested in stocks or bonds or other types of investments. Because of this exclusion, the Default Rules take over and states that approximately 50% of the assets be invested in Bonds and 50% in Stocks.

Many grantors would be surprised to learn that because they did not stipulate investment percentage, their trustee, in following the Default Rules, will be required to sell most of their individual stocks that go into their Trust and to purchase bonds or bond funds and stock mutual funds in order to obtain proper diversification. This is especially true for equity investments under the new Uniform Prudent Investor Act (UPIA). See Appendix F.

For Income to be Paid:

> Remember what most Trusts state:
>
> "My trustee is to pay my surviving spouse the net income form the trust."

If you do not say how much annual income you or your surviving spouse are to receive from the Trust, the Default Rules will determine those payments. The income payments will be based on current interest and dividend rates.

An example is shown below based on the fact that the Trusts did not state how the funds were to be invested, nor the income to be paid.

If one of the spouses were to die in 2001, then the funds would be invested as follows and the income that could be expected is shown.

Low income from a "Balanced Trust" (a Default Rule)

Type of Investment	Investments %	Amount	Gross Annual Income %[11]	Amount
Good Quality Medium Term Bond Fund	50%	$ 337,500	6.0%	$ 20,250
Good Quality Growth Stock Fund	50%	337,500	0.9%	3,038.
TOTAL		$ 675,000		$ 23,288
Less Half of the Fees and Expenses of the Trusts				- 3,510
NET INCOME FROM TRUST				$ 19,778

A "Net Income" provision is found in most Trusts. A grantor may believe that there will be little or no expense for their Trust since they are using a family member or friend as trustee. But, there will be expenses for annual tax reports to the state and federal government; legal and other professional services. A family member or friend who is trustee should evaluate the benefits of delegating the investment responsibility. The new Uniform Prudent Investor Act (Appendix F) relieves the trustee of legal liability if the investment decisions are properly delegated. If this is not done, the Act places new requirements on the trustee that will probably add to the annual cost of the trusteeship. The assistance of a Trust attorney, especially in the beginning years of the Trust, will be needed. This is discussed in more detail in Chapter 9 and in Appendix B.

The important point to remember is that under the Default Rules the income payments to the surviving spouse are limited to the actual interest and dividends received and generally reduced by a portion of the fees and expenses of the trust.

Our position is that the income needs may exceed the actual income received by the Trust. Therefore, the grantor, when stating a higher annual income payment, requires the trustee to take this additional amount from the principal of the Trust. Based on the estimates, this removal may come from the gains in the growth of the assets held by the Trust and thereby not cause a decrease in the value of the Trust.

Avoid Trusts that Pay Net Income

Most Trusts state that the "Net Income" is to be paid to your surviving spouse or other income beneficiary. If you have a Trust, it probably says this. Why?

The "Net Income" provision reduces the income to be paid to the surviving spouse. In the majority of cases, as indicated in this book, the exact amount of annual income, increased for inflation is what should be clearly stated in the document that established the Trust. As the grantor you also have the right to state that the "Gross Income" will be paid. For additional information on this option, see Chapter 10.

How the use of net income changed from early English law to its current use in the United Sates is very interesting.

Old English law controlling estate planning

Many of our laws came from England. Over four hundred years ago the wealthy gentry were the lords and barons who held vast lands. When they died, their Trusts stated: after provisions were made for: the payments to and upkeep of their overseers, servants and peasants who worked the land; reserves for repairs and the purchase of the seed for next year's harvest and the grain and other feed for the livestock, what was then left over was "the net income" and was to be paid to the income beneficiaries

We have modified this concept from English law. The legal rule in our country (based on the Uniform Principal and Income Act) is that if the Trust states "Net Income" is to be paid to the income beneficiaries, then half of the costs of managing, filing required annual reports with the federal and state governments and other expenses of the Trusts are charged against the Gross Income of the Trust. The other half of the Trust's expenses are charged against the principal of the Trust. The Net Income provision can reduce the income paid to the surviving spouse by as much as 10% a year. Additional information, including examples of why the selection of the Gross Income or the Net Income provision should be made by the Grantor of the Trust, is in Chapter 10.

With this information on Trust investments and net income, let's take a look at what happened to the Wilsons who established Credit Shelter Trusts because they heard they could save at least $235,000 in federal estate taxes.

John incorrectly believed that state and federal

laws controlled his estate after his death and that he had no financial options. Because of this misconception, he first considered using a preprinted legal form for his estate plan. Later, he shopped around for an attorney who would prepare his estate planning documents for the lowest fixed fee. He selected an attorney based on the recommendation of a friend. John and his wife met with the attorney who agreed to prepare their estate planning documents for a fixed amount. When they met, the attorney asked the names of the children, his trustee and a few other items.

John never asked if he had financial options to consider. His emphasis was on the cost to prepare what he called "simple documents." A few weeks later, he received drafts of the documents.

In reviewing them, John read many pages that continually referred to sections of the federal revenue code and other laws. He finally decided that all he needed to do with the documents was to determine that the names of his spouse, his children and the trustee were correct. Everything else, John incorrectly assumed, was controlled by various state and federal laws regarding Trusts. His assumption was a mistake. Like many other financially uninformed grantors, he did not realize that he could and should exercise control of his money. He did not think of his Trust as an investment. John should have realized that he had many financial and management options that he should consider to properly provide for his wife, Mary, and for their children. If he had made these decisions and correctly expressed them in the Trust, it could have made a big difference to his wife and children.

The mistake of not being aware of the financial options was in part, the fault of John and his wife. They never asked what income the surviving spouse would receive from the Trust after the death of one of them. They were aware that if one of them died in 2001, $675,000 of their assets would go into a Trust. (In 2006, they can put $1 million, of assets in the Trust) And, they also knew that the surviving spouse could receive a lifetime income from the Trust.

John and Mary Wilson mistakenly assumed that a sufficient amount would be paid. They also assumed that what was written into their Trust was what was required by law. For the Wilsons these were incorrect assumptions and they remain incorrect for the rest of us.   The question John and Mary needed to ask themselves was: "What income will the surviving spouse need from the Trust?" The Trust department of a bank could have told them the current interest rate on bonds and the   average   dividend percent on good quality   growth stocks.   With this information they could have quickly determined the amount of income that would be received and is shown on page 62.

Even through the amounts that can be placed into Credit Shelter Trusts will increase to $1 million in the year 2006, the income payments under the Default Rules will continue to be low.

John and Mary Wilson needed to determine if the income   from their Credit Shelter Trusts would be sufficient for either of them to live on after the death of the other. Determining needed   income   is   not complicated to do. By using Exhibit 1 "Income Needs of Each Spouse" John and Mary could determine the

IF YOU DON'T WANT
TO CHECK-IN AS A
BAG LADY . . .
CHECK-OUT THE
INCOME
YOU WILL RECEIVE
FROM
YOUR HUSBAND'S
TRUST!

amount required from the Trust.

With the information you now have, this would be an opportune time for you and your spouse to take a few minutes and each complete your own copy of Exhibits 1 and 2. Remove the copies, at the back of the book to use as work sheets. Make copies for each person and follow the instructions for completing Exhibits 1 & 2 in Appendix G.

Both John and Mary Wilson followed this procedure. It was then that they discovered their already established Trusts did not properly meet the income needs of either one of them.

1.   Mary will need $34,950 in 2001 from her husband's Credit Shelter Trust if he died in 2001. But as indicated on Page 56, the "Net Income Paid" from a Trust controlled by the Default Rules will be $19,778 in 2001. This amount is significantly below Mary's needs.

2.   This shortage of income from the Trust for Mary Wilson will continue throughout her lifetime if her husband dies first. This is shown below in column four, below. (Note: In four out of five marriages, husbands die first).

Mary Wilson's income shortage as a widow:

Years after Husband's Death	Actual Trust Payments	Required Annual Payments	Mary's Shortage Of Income
1st Year	$ 19,778	$ 35,000	$15,222
5th Year	20,156	39,393	19,237
10th Year	20,810	45,667	24,857

3.   John will need $19,950 in 2000 from his wife's Credit Shelter Trust if she died in 2001. And, as indicated on **Page 41**, even with trustee fees and expenses, the approximate Net Income appears to meet John's needs - at least in 2001. But this is not the case in later years. The increase in the cost of inflation could cause John Wilson to receive from the Trust less than he needs.

4.   The differences between John's needs from the Trust and Mary's needs is the pension payment. There would be a $15,000 reduction to his widow if John dies first. In some cases the pension payments terminate upon the death of the husband. This is particularly true in many cases if a second marriage takes place after the husband has retired and is already receiving his pension.

Let's Look at the Revision of John's Trust for the benefit of Mary based on her Income Needs. Your Trust, May Require the Same Type of Revisions for Your Surviving Spouse

A.   John stated in his Trust that his wife was to receive $35,000 on the date his Trust was executed (2000) if he died in that year. And,

B.   That this amount was to be increased for inflation each year starting in the next year and continuing each year during Mary's lifetime.

John wanted a method to test the ability of his Credit Shelter Trust to provide this annual income to

Mary. He wanted to know first if there would be enough funds in the Trust to provide the income, and what the value of the Trust would be during Mary's life. John also wanted to know what mix of bonds and stocks would best provide the income for his wife and then leave funds for their children upon Mary's death.

How this was done is presented in Appendix H.

<u>What you must do</u>

1.   You must determine the income needs of you and your surviving spouse. To do this, use Exhibits 1 and 2. Copies are in the back of this book.

2.   The amount required should be for the current year. Place this amount in your Trust. Next, increase it from that date for inflation. The amount required should be stated in an exhibit to the Trust. This will allow for the ease of later changes when the Trust is reviewed at least every five years.

3.   You need to test the ability of the Trust to increase in value and pay the income requirements. This is done by assumptions you make on the increased value of stocks over your estimate of the life of the Trust. A method to do this is presented in Appendix H.

Surviving Spouse Still head of the Family?

Most trusts say "NO"

The law has traditionally treated women as second-class citizens. And now many Trusts treat both the husband and the wife as second-class citizens. This practice of considering the surviving spouse as incompetent appears in estate planning documents and Trusts. And since four out of five men die first in a marriage, the wife, as the surviving spouse is the one most victimized by this practice, when she becomes a widow.

Most wives would be better served if they used their right to engage their own attorney to represent them when estate plans are being prepared. Or better yet, first consult with a qualified financial planner trained and experience in the issues presented in this book.

Wives could then require adequate consideration not only of their needs but of their position as the remaining head of the family vs. estate planning documents that do not consider or provide for their needs and treat them as persons not capable of managing their own affairs.

Poor IRS Regulation

This concept of incompetency of the surviving spouse reaches into our government. It is seen in IRS regulations regarding so-called "Sprinkling Powers" discussed later in this Chapter

Make surviving spouse the head of the family

Do not allow the documents to list yourself, man or women, as second class citizens. Remember you have the right to override the default rules, not to be trapped by outdated legal thinking and practices and you have the right to avoid IRS regulations. Some of these regulations appear to restrict, in estate planning documents, the surviving spouse's capabilities to remain the head of the family.

You can exercise your right by giving directives in your documents that clearly establish the surviving spouse's authority. Examples of the most common key areas where this issue needs to be clarified are presented below.

You need to use this knowledge of your rights to determine what are the other special areas, based on your family and their needs, that should be clearly addressed in your documents.

Bad advice causes family problems

You would expect that attorneys and others who give advice on estate planning know what you are legally allowed to do and have some appreciation of your concerns and objectives. But in many instances, this does not appear to be the case.

Law schools do not cover these important financial and management options in their courses in estate planning. Most attorney malpractice insurance policies exclude coverage for attorneys who give investment advice. And, once an attorney starts to talk

HENRY OF
HAPPY
MEMORY

HIS TRUST
ALLOWED
HIS WIFE
TO HELP
THEIR
CHILDREN

about income needs of the surviving spouse and what returns can be expected from investments in a trust, that attorney rightly becomes concerned about losing malpractice coverage.

This is one of the reasons, if you do need help, to consider the services of a financially trained person with training and experience in estate planning, prior to meeting with your attorney. By the time you do get to the attorney, you should have explicit knowledge of how your assets will be distributed and the financial and management instructions for their use. Your planner should be present at your meeting with the attorney.

Power to distribute the income of the Trust

Most grantors would like their Trust to distribute the Trust income to their wife and children based on their needs.

Once attorneys hear this as an objective of a grantor, they immediately say, "This is called 'Sprinkling Powers' and is permitted under IRS regulations." And, you are advised that the IRS code does not permit the surviving spouse to have this power. The IRS code does allow a trustee, other than the surviving spouse, to have the power to distribute the income or to hold all or part of the income and reinvest it.

The statement that only the trustee can have this power and not the surviving spouse is not true. The surviving spouse *can* have this power. The only thing the IRS code does to restrict the surviving spouse's

CHILDREN NEED MONEY NOW ..
NOT TEN OR MORE YEARS FROM NOW.
Your Trust can Provide for This.

authority is to require that all of the income must be
distributed that year if the surviving spouse has power.

Trustees cause Family Problems

On a practical basis, giving certain authorities
to a trustee, instead of to the surviving spouse, can
cause problems. Consider the following regarding the
distribution of Trust income.

1.   Each of the beneficiaries of the Trust can contest what the trustee decides. Therefore, the professional trustee must carefully document any decision to distribute income. The trustee must continually gather financial information from the children and the spouse before determining how much income, if any, each will receive each year. This additional work of a professional trustee may result in extra fees (taken from the Trust). Decisions to withhold income is almost always the safest course for a trustee.

2.   In the case where a family member is trustee, the results can be damaging. At best it will create strains within the family. How does a son or daughter determine the proper allocation each year among their parent, their siblings and themselves? What documentation must the family member trustee obtain to properly make the annual decisions and document these decisions against later arguments and perhaps even lawsuits within the family?

3.   High income tax rates are charged on income held in the Trust. If a trustee, other than the surviving spouse uses their authority to not distribute all or any part of the income, that income is taxed in the Trust at very high rates. And, it will take years of investment growth to reach its original pre-tax value. The beneficiaries of the Trust will be better served if they had these funds now and could invest in a home or some other worthwhile endeavor.

Surviving spouse best judge of needs

The surviving spouse is probably a better judge of what is right for the children and should be relied upon to make such decisions.

The trustee is then relieved of the responsibility of gathering information and documenting decisions. The trustee will be following the instructions of the surviving spouse.

The only loss of options in giving this power is that the surviving spouse cannot direct the trustee to hold any part of the income in the Trust. All of the income must be distributed each year when the surviving spouse has this power. But this is a much better option - distributing all of the income now instead of having the funds withheld for many years.

A contingent provision can be made if, later in life, the surviving spouse is no longer competent to make sensible distributions.

Consider giving authority to direct that the funds be distributed from a separate Trust for the benefit of any child or other heir based on the decision of the surviving spouse.

Giving the surviving spouse the power to distribute the income preserves the concept of the parent as the head of the family.

The strength of family relationships, after the death of the grantor, can be enhanced by directives in the Trust that considers the children and gives authority to the surviving spouse to include them as recipients of the annual income from the Trust.

Power to give principal to the children

The same question arises regarding the distribution of principal from the Trust. Who should have the power to distribute principal from the Trust during the surviving spouse's lifetime- - the trustee or the surviving spouse?

A refinement to this question is required based on federal tax law. If the trust is a Credit Shelter Trust, which is the basic Trust for married couples, the surviving spouse should not have authority to invade the principal of the Trust for his or her own benefit above that amount permitted under the "5 & 5" power (discussed in Chapter 11).

To do so causes problems with the tax-exempt status of the trust - which was the reason why it was created.

However, and this is important, the surviving spouse can have the power to direct the trustee to give funds to the children and other remaindermen from the principal of the Trust.

Do not exclude your children

Every Credit Shelter Trust and most Marital Trusts completely exclude the children prior to the death of the surviving spouse. Why? Unfortunately the answer is, "because it has always been done that way." Not good enough. In many cases there are excess funds in the Trust that can be distributed to the children during the surviving spouse's lifetime.

I'D LIKE TO HELP EDUCATE MY GRANDSON,
BUT YOUR FATHER'S TRUST LEFT ME WITH A
LIMITED INCOME AND NO AUTHORITY TO
RELEASE FUNDS TO YOU. . . WAIT UNTIL I DIE
AND THEN YOU'LL HAVE LOTS OF MONEY.

Giving your surviving spouse the right to distribute both income and principal to the children will greatly aid family relationships.

Children need money today, not ten or twenty years from now. Surviving spouses are now living into their late eighties and nineties. Their children are over sixty and most are retired when the surviving parent dies. The grandchildren too, are in their forties.

Think of the need and benefit for these children and the grandchildren. Think of the joy the surviving spouse experiences when, as head of the family, that person can see a need and then provide some funds for the children or grandchildren from the Trust.

No longer will the surviving parent be forced to say, "I wish I could help you buy a home or educate my grandchild, but I have limited funds and your father forgot to include a provision in his trust that would allow you to receive some funds while I am alive. Wait until I die and then you'll have lots of money."

The surviving spouse with authority to distribute funds can maintain strong family relationships.

Limitations to protect your spouse

When the Trust empowers the surviving spouse, there are certain issues to consider. The surviving spouse can have the authority to determine the distribution of both income and principal. But due to a technicality of the law, while the authority to distribute principal should be written separately from the authority to distribute income. This is another example where you must first state what you want to have happen˙ Your attorney will then be able to properly address the issue and write the directives that will conform to any existing laws and regulations.

Authority to distribute income

Tell your attorney that you want your surviving spouse to have the authority to direct the trustee to distribute all or any portion of the income to any one or more of a group consisting of the children, other heirs and themselves. This amount can be paid directly to those designated or held in Trust for their benefit, as the surviving spouse, in his or her discretion, may determine.

Authority to distribute principal

The authority to distribute principal should be subject to certain limitations. For example, distributions might only be authorized when the Credit Shelter Trust is above certain values. This is used to make sure the surviving spouse does not give away funds that may be needed later. An initial amount can be selected and can be indexed to increase for inflation or increase annually at a certain percentage.

You can also state these conditions in absolute amounts. You can stipulate whenever the value of the Trust is over a certain amount or, when it is indicated that surplus funds are in the Trust, you want these funds distributed. A method is required to determine how to calculate surplus funds in the Trust.. It is not difficult to do and should be clearly stated in your Trust.

You can also consider this requirement that when any distribution of the principal of the Trust is to be made, it must be made equally to each child, but may be held in a Trust for one or more of the children as directed by the surviving spouse.

CHAPTER 9

Who Should be Your Trustee?

Duties of a Trustee

Selecting your trustee requires careful planning and consideration of the work a trustee does. The work your trustee does is different from that of your executor.[1] The main responsibility of a trustee is the investment management of the assets in your Trust. Next, the trustee must know the laws regarding Trusts and properly administer the Trust according to the terms and conditions you have clearly stated in your Trust. All of your trustee's actions must faithfully follow the directives in your Trust - the "Duty of Loyalty" is a very strong and well defined legal obligation, the technical and legal aspects of which are not understood

---

(1) An executor is a person appointed in a Will to carry out directives in the Will. These directives generally include burial instructions, the payment of debts, disposing of personal property and distributing the remaining assets as provided for in the Will. If assets are to be placed in a Trust, the Will names the Trust as the primary beneficiary and the executor gives these assets to the trustee. In addition, since a Will goes through the probate process, an executor is responsible for this and it is generally accomplished by hiring an attorney.

An executor's responsibility is to protect and preserve the assets of the deceased that are contained in the Will. The executor is not to invest these assets in securities other than in short-term investments that preserve the capital, such as savings accounts. A trustee does invest in securities and is governed by the directives in the Trust, Trust law and Trust case law.

by most trustees.[2] And your trustee must know and follow the "Default Rules" of the state in areas where general instructions are given or the particular issue is not addressed in your document.

Annually your trustee must arrange for the filing of state and federal fiduciary tax returns. The above are the main duties of a trustee.

The care, advice and comfort given to your surviving spouse are best given by family members and friends. There is no requirement that only a trustee is required to do this for the surviving spouse. A professional trustee can provide some of this type of assistance when a nursing home or other care is required. But again, family members can best handle this and look to the trustee to pay the bills, if needed.

Yet, given the above, most Trusts use a family member or a friend as their trustee. Why? Is it because the family member or friend has the training and experience in investments, normally devotes time to this activity and can be relied upon to manage the investments better than a professional trustee? And is there any guarantee that the family member or friend will faithfully follow the directives or the "Default Rules" of the state?

"No, this is not the case" is the answer given in the majority of situations. We tend to use a family member or friend as our trustee to compensate for the

(2)   As an example, a trustee may believe their action proper if they were the highest bidder for the purchase of real estate owned by the Trust. But, they should have obtained permission of the court to do so.

stories we have heard over the years (some true, most not true) about banks as trustees. We also do not want to pay the fees banks or other professionals charge.

The case for having a family member as your trustee should not be based purely on the expense of professional trustee's fees. These fees can be low, sometimes less than one percent of the value of the assets (see Appendix E). And the Trust can state that family members can negotiate lower trustee fees.

Most of us, as grantors, never think about it, but when we select a family member as trustee we are also saying that the person can do an equal or better job of investing the Trust assets than professional investment managers. This is seldom true.

The investment results when a family member is trustee seldom matches that of the professional trustee. The fees can be more than offset by the investment performance of professional trustees.

The information presented in this book will alert you to the issues of current-day Trust management. Some of the negative stories you have heard resulted from past laws that greatly restricted all trustees, including banks. But most of these past problems were caused by attorneys who used boilerplate provisions in the documents.

Laws on investing Trust assets

Most of the investment options a trustee has came about through changes in the types of securities approved by regulatory authorities for Trusts. Prior to World War II, bonds of high quality were to be held by trustees. In the thirties, high quality investment grade bonds paid a low interest rate of about 2.0% to 2.5%. Growth stocks were not held in Trusts unless the grantor gave specific instructions, which rarely happened.

Many states had "legal lists" of securities a trustee could invest in. After World War II, a small portion of high quality stocks were approved for Trusts. Even then, many states' legal lists did not approve investing in mutual funds. The holding of stocks, as approved trustee investments, has steadily increased since then. Now about 50 percent stock holdings are considered reasonable and appropriate for a "Balanced Trust" to provide fairly for the lifetime income beneficiary as well as for the remaindermen.

Investing under the new Uniform Prudent Investors Act (UPIA) [3] is based on "modern portfolio theory" and requires wide diversification in stocks. Mutual funds and index funds can provide this diversification.

Stories that circulated in the past about the low income a person received from a Trust were true and it can still occur today, at typical interest and dividend rates, if a person does not use their options to state the income the surviving spouse or other income beneficiary is to receive.

(3)　　The new Uniform Prudent Investor Act (UPIA) rewards your family trustee by relieving them of future liability for investment results if a professional trustee is properly selected. See Appendix F, Section 9.

Very few Trusts had provisions for quickly and simply removing a trustee. Part of these changes that make it easier for the surviving spouse, or another family member, to remove and replace a trustee are the result of recent tax court rulings.

Myths about trustees

Separate laws and regulations do not exist for different kinds of trustees, one for professional trustees and another for those trustees who are family members or friends. The same regulations, laws, and case law apply for all trustees.

The courts do hold professional trustees more strictly accountable, such as banks, since they hold themselves out to the public as having greater knowledge in Trust management and investing.

A family member or friend serving as trustee must follow the laws for Trusts including the Default Rules of their state. This is why it is strongly recommended that a family member trustee seek the advice of a Trust attorney before acting as the trustee.

Key issues to consider

1. How long will the Trust last?

Knowing how long a Trust will need to last is the first issue to look at when selecting a trustee. The issue is very important when the grantor does not select the Trust department of a bank or a brokerage firm as their trustee. If a bank or a brokerage firm is selected, the question does not need to be addressed since these trustees can be expected to be in business during the full life of the Trust.

Many Grantors select a relative or friend to be the trustee of their Trust. One or more successor trustees are also named. Generally those selected as trustees and successor trustees have traditionally been in their late forties or older with was no provision in the documentation for either the income beneficiary, heirs or the current trustee to name a successor trustee.

The following example would apply to most couples establishing Credit Shelter Trusts and clearly indicates that this important issue is generally not properly addressed.

Assume that a Trust was established when a man was 60 years of age and his wife was, for purposes of this example, 56 years of age. Based on a normal life time expectancy, the husband might die first at age 80 or older.

This means that the man's Credit Shelter Trust would become operative 20 years after he signed his Trust and designated his trustee. His wife might live until age 88 or 90 years of age. This indicates that the Trustee will be required for at least 35 to 40 years after the signing of the Trust.

Selecting a 45 year-old person as your trustee assumes that this person would be alive and be capable of serving as trustee when past the age 85. The incapacities of later years need to be considered.

Many Trusts name one of the children as trustee. If that son or daughter was age 30 or 35 when the grantor was 60 years old, assumes that the person named trustee would be alive and capable of serving when past 65 years of age. Perhaps this is a reasonable assumption, but successors are also required. A bank could be the final successor.

When a successor trustee has been named, the same test applies. How old will the successor trustees be 35 to 40 years from now. Will they also be competent and able to serve during the life of the Trust?

Many Trusts do not include the provision that the surviving spouse or other designees name successor trustees. One solution is to add such a provision that allows your spouse or others to do this.   This recommendation is also in line with the other part of this issue, that your spouse (or someone else) should have the power to remove the trustee.

An alternative recommendation is for the trustee to be given authority to name his or her own successor.

It may be possible that the income beneficiary be able to terminate a trustee and name a new one. An alternative is for the surviving spouse to terminate the trustee and for one of the children (a Remainderman) to name the new one. One can also consider a provision for one of the heirs to have the authority to terminate the trustee and appoint the successor in the event that the income beneficiary becomes incapacitated,

A brief summary of the duties and responsibilities of trustees is in Appendix B. It is very important that these items be discussed with the individuals the grantor has named as trustees. Sometimes the person who had said they would serve as trustee, has asked not to be named a trustee after their duties and responsibilities were reviewed with them. And, in a many cases, after learning of the investment duties and responsibilities of their trustee(s), the grantor themselves changed the person they originally selected.

2. Co-trustees -- issues and problems

Many Trusts use "Co-trustees" such as a bank and a son or daughter or other relatives of the grantor. Perhaps this was suggested by the preparer of the Trust in response to the grantor's desire to have a family member oversee the acts of the bank or brokerage firm serving as a trustee. Two family members may also be selected as Co-trustees.

When you name Co-trustees you are requiring that the trustees must act together - that both are in agreement as to the actions/decisions made in the handling of the investments in the Trust as well as other matters provided for in the document. If one Co-trustee does not agree, nothing can be done.

When a professional trustee is selected as a trustee, along with a family member, it is generally the professional trustee who makes all of the investment recommendations. Before they are implemented, the professional trustee obtains the agreement, in writing, of the other Co-trustee.

At first this may sound to the grantor to be exactly what they want - a family member approving every action of the professional investment manager. Or, two family members being in agreement on all investment matters and decisions affecting the surviving spouse, the children, and the other heirs.

Rarely does a family member, as Co-trustee, make investment recommendations to the professional investment manager serving as the other Co-trustee.

Often the two family member Co-trustees cannot agree to sell or buy a security. Then, nothing is done - which in itself is an investment decision.

As an example of this problem, Mary Burns, a niece, was named Co-trustee with a major bank in Florida. During the entire 10-year-life of the Trust, Mary never approved any investment change recommended by the bank. She knew nothing about investments and felt that the original stocks held by her Uncle Harry should not be changed. She did not want to be criticized by other nieces and nephews for selling or buying any securities after their aunt, Uncle Harry's wife, died. Mary's thoughts were if Uncle Harry believed Pennsylvania Railroad, now bankrupt, was a good stock to own, we will not sell it, despite what the bank recommends.

No grantor wants a Mary Burns type of Co-trustee. Yet bank Trust officers who attend my CLE (Continuing Legal Education) class state that they have these problems with about 5% of their Co-trustees (but not as bad as the Florida bank had with "Cousin Mary"). A few banks have stated that their procedure is to advise the Co-trustee that if this lack of cooperation is to continue, the bank will resign as trustee. In some of these cases, the courts would then select the replacement trustee for the bank if the document did not contain a provision for selecting another bank as a replacement trustee

We could continue with many other examples of problems with Co-trustees. Many times the Co-trustee concept is less efficient in the management of the Trust's investments. In too many cases this can, over time, result in investment losses in the Trust, reduced income to the lifetime income beneficiary, and a lower value of Trust assets for the remaindermen.

Consider a "Special Trustee"

You can provide in your Trust for a "Special Trustee(s)" such as family members or friends whose responsibilities are clearly stated in the Trust and are different from the traditional role of a trustee. These "Special Trustee(s)" would have responsibilities such as, caring for, advising and giving comfort to your surviving spouse or other income beneficiaries.

If a nursing home or other medical care is required for the surviving spouse or other income beneficiaries, this person would visit the nursing home to ensure that proper care was be given. This special trustee could also have the Health Care Power of Attorney. Funds can be provided from the Trust for compensating this person and reasonable expenses could be provided also for gifts, travel expenses, etc. if needed.

3. The Work Trustees Perform.

Before you quickly decide who will be your trustee or co-trustees, first look at the work required and any professional qualifications needed to do the work your trustee(s) are expected to perform.

A.   Management of the Assets in the Trust

The most important single thing a trustee does is to properly manage the investments of the assets placed in the Trust. This must be done carefully and by people with knowledge and experience in investing. This requires much time and is not in any way a casual activity.

Because of past investment problems in Trusts, the new Uniform Prudent Investors Act (UPIA) was written. A copy of this new law is in Appendix F. Since this is a uniform act it has already become the law in many States and is scheduled for adoption by many other states. If your state has not adopted it, you can have written into your Trust key provisions of the Act that you want included.

You also have the right in your Trust to expand upon, restrict, eliminate or otherwise alter provisions of this new law (UPIA).

You should examine the Default Rules of your state which are separate from the provisions of the new Uniform Prudent Investors Act (UPIA) and consider those you want to override.

To further clarify the above, let me use as an

example the following:

A.   The Default Rules of most states require the trustee, when the Trust is silent as to how the funds are to be invested, to invest the assets into what is called a Balanced Trust that favors neither your spouse nor your children. This is generally interpreted as placing 50% of the assets in bonds and 50% of the assets in stock.

B.   You should give serious thought to overriding this Default Rule. Consider placing a much higher percentage into good quality growth stocks. Consider stating the annual income to be paid to your spouse by using many other options available to you and presented in this book.

C.   The new Uniform Prudent Investors Act (UPIA) provides standards for investing the assets in the Trust. We recommend overriding the Default Rules of a state that says 50% of the assets be invested in bonds. We do not recommend overriding the investment concepts under UPIA.

A professional investment manager should be considered for the management of the investment duties of a trustee. Also consider giving your spouse the right to replace this trustee.

Under Section 9 of the new Uniform Prudent Investors Act (UPIA), a family member or friend is motivated to hire such a professional investment manager. This law breaks new ground. It relieves the trustee of any future liability resulting from investments of Trust funds if the investment authority is properly delegated under the new law.

It is not sensible to name a family member or friend as your trustee just to save the small fee of a professional investment manager. Start reviewing the investment results of several professional trustees. Most banks publish this data and will give this information to you free.

Avoiding a small fee for a professional investment manager by naming a family member or friend as your trustee may not result in any saving. Your family member will incur brokerage fees, legal costs and other expenses. The provisions of Section 9 of the new Uniform Prudent Investors Act (UPIA) encourage your trustee to engage a qualified professional trustee, someone you could have selected.

I recommend you review this new law; and along with it, a few comments regarding it in Appendix F. Review also the types and fees of professional investment managers contained in Appendix E. You may want to reconsider your position in this matter.

Other duties of your trustee

Your trustee(s) has also been given the power to provide additional funds from the principal of the Trust necessary or proper for your spouse's maintenance, support, care, comfort, well being and general welfare.

How frequent will it be necessary to provide additional funds from the principal of your Trust?

If your Trust is like many , it may not utilize your

options to properly provide for the income your spouse requires. As a result, your trustee will continually receive requests for additional funds.

Professional trustees will require full and complete documentation and justification of such request for additional funds. If a family member is a trustee, they may or may not quickly agree to the request for additional funds. Your family trustee will also be required to properly document the justification for agreeing to provide such funds.

Reasons for proper documentation of requests for additional funds are many and must be valid. Professional trustees know this and the future legal problems that can occur by not doing the documentation.

If you have a family member as your trustee, future legal and tax problems can result if payment of additional funds from the principal are made without proper justification. Without properly prepared documentation, it can be very difficult years later for a family trustee to justify why they gave $50,000 out of the principal, ten years before.

This is another reason why I recommend that a family member or friend consult an experienced Trust attorney immediately when the Trust is activated. Otherwise mistakes will be made by the trustee that can result in legal, financial and tax problems. For additional information on the duties of a trustee, see Appendix B.

Being available to the surviving spouse to answer

questions and assist in the surviving spouse's needs is something grantors like to think their trustee will do. As mentioned earlier, this is generally done best by family members and friends.

Be careful in assuming that a professional trustee will be available to do this work or any part of it. Today professional trustees are investment mangers. A few banks in major locations still have a person in their Trust department who will try to assist the income beneficiary.   However, this   practice has been disappearing in the Trust activities of banks.

Brokerage firms have recently entered into this business by establishing wholly owned Trust banks. While they have strong representation through their broker network, I have seen no indication of their using their large sales force to increase their Trust business among grantors about 80% of whom do not use a professional trustee..

Terminating the trustee

Your surviving spouse or another person should always have the authority to terminate a trustee, especially a professional trustee, and to select a replacement. If your spouse should move after your death to another state to be near your children, there should be the option of selecting a new trustee convenient to the new residence.

Generally, families rely on their children or friends to provide assistance to the surviving spouse. There is a strong need for this especially as the survivor advances in age. Medical needs increase. Nursing homes may eventually be required.

Few Trusts properly consider the needs of the surviving spouse in later years. In many cases, family members no longer even live in the same area. Children and other family members or friends can be miles apart.

Provision should be considered in your Trust to pay the expenses for those at a distance to visit the surviving spouse in their later years, to offer comfort and to ensure that they are receiving proper care.

EXAMINE YOUR CURRENT TRUST CAREFULLY
- DOES IT INCLUDE KEY OPTIONS
TO PROTECT AND PROPERLY
PROVIDE FOR YOUR FAMILY?

Increasing the End-Value of Your Trust For Your Children

<u>Directives you can give</u>

Directives can be given to invest a major portion or all of the assets in good quality growth stocks. This is done based on the grantor's knowledge of the long-term benefits of investing in stocks and of the affects of inflation over the years.

Inflation destroys the future purchasing power of funds invested in fixed income securities such as bonds, Certificates of Deposit, etc. Yet this concept was not recognized in Trusts. Traditionally 50% was invested in bonds under the Default Rules. And as the other 50% invested in stocks grew in value, stocks were sold to buy bonds and maintain the 50% bond mix. The income from the bonds is given to the surviving spouse, leaving the bond principal to decline in purchasing power. This can be seen in the simple comparison below of the increase in the cost to mail a letter a first-class letter.

3 cents   34 cents
1958   2001

<u>Inflation</u>
1,033 % increase

Many people know the home their parents purchased for $12,000 in 1949 is now worth over $200,000 - a much higher rate of inflation than the cost of a first-class stamp. But many Trusts do not protect against the effects of inflation.

You can give directives to protect against a loss in the purchasing power of the assets in your Trust caused by inflation. This is done by giving directives to invest the assets in good quality growth stocks. This chapter will tell how you can give additional directives to further increase the value of your Trust for your children and other heirs. Providing funds to be given to your children during your spouse's life should also be considered. How to do this was presented in Chapter 8.

If a couple has assets valued above their combined federal estate-tax exemptions,[1] there are several additional directives, presented in this chapter, that can be give in Credit Shelter Trusts. These directives can increase the end-value of the Credit Shelter Trust for the heirs.

The Credit Shelter Trust holds the funds that can be inherited by your children and others without any federal estate tax. This amount for each individual

(1)   When a couple's assets exceed their combined estate-tax credit, the additional assets can be given tax free to the surviving spouse or placed in a tax-free Marital Trust. These additional assets would be used first for the support of the surviving spouse. Directives are then given that will provide for the maximum growth in value of these tax-free funds in the Credit Shelter Trust for the benefit of the children and other heirs.

Grantor is currently $675,000 in 2001 and will increase to $1 million starting in the year 2006.

It is possible, over the remaining lifetime of the surviving spouse, to have the value of such a Trust increase to over $10 million.

The general rule is:

As you give directives to increase the end-value of your Credit Shelter Trust for your children and other heirs, you decrease the income from the Trust for your surviving spouse.

When the income to the surviving spouse is being reduced, a safety net should be in the Trust to provide additional funds if the surviving spouse needs them at some future time. This "Safety Net" method is shown in Chapter 11, "Extra Money When You Need It"

Parents with one child may think that increasing the end-value of the Trust is not important. Their child may receive a sizeable estate, of up to $2 million tax free, upon the death of both parents. For parents of a larger family increasing the end-value of the Trust is more important particularly when they want to provide as much as possible for the children and other heirs.

Not everyone needs money from the Trust

As an Example, Robert, age 66, and Jane Mathews, age 65, have a current net worth of about $2.4 million. They have four children and seven grandchildren. Robert receives a generous pension and upon his death, Jane will continue to receive a major part of it.

Included in the listing of their assets, below, is a total of $1,350,000 in stocks and stock mutual funds. This value is estimated, at a conservative annual growth of 8% a year, to increase to about $2,000,000 in five years and about $2,900,000 in ten years. If all the other assets did not increase, including the value of their home, their estate in ten years would be worth about $4.0 million and subject to large estate taxes. To mitigate this - Robert and Jane Mathews planned to annually review the growth of their estate and consider additional estate planning strategies. (These strategies are discussed in later chapters.)

Home - Jointly owned with		
right of survivorship		$350,000
In Jane's name:		
-Stocks & Mutual Funds	$ 550,000	
-CDs, Bonds, Savings Accounts	250,000	
Sub Total		800,000
In Robert's name:		
-Stocks & Mutual Funds	$ 800,000	
-CDs, Bonds, Savings Accounts	250,000	
Sub Total		1,050,000
Other Assets:		
-Life Insurance, Face Value		
payable to Jane	$200,000	
-Cars, Jewelry, home		
furnishings, etc.	50,000	
Sub Total		250,000
Total		$ 2,450,000

The Mathews' current goal is to increase the end-value of their Credit Shelter Trusts for the benefit of their four children.

Their prior estate planning documents included Living Trusts to avoid probate and to take advantage of their individual federal estate-tax exemptions. Their Living Trusts were properly funded. The balance of their individual estates passed tax free to the surviving spouse by the use of the marital deduction.

If Robert died in the current year, 2001, $675,000 would be placed in his Credit Shelter Trust. The balance of their assets would go to his wife Jane. As a result, Jane would have a net worth of $1,825,000 in 2001.

If Robert died ten years later, $1 million would go into his Credit Shelter Trust. After this deduction, Jane would have a net worth of about $3,000,000 based on the increase in their stocks from $1,350,000 to $2,900,000. The same basic amounts would apply to Robert's net worth, if Jane died first. Therefore, there was no need of income for the surviving spouse from the Credit Shelter Trust each had established.

The surviving spouse would not need income from the Credit Shelter Trust. It would just add more taxable income for the surviving spouse. The living expenses and other needs would be paid from the earnings and growth of their capital. For family reasons, the Mathews did not want to leave the money from their federal estate-tax exemption directly to their children at their death.

Each of the Mathews' Living Trusts were "silent" as to income and investments. Each Trust stated that the surviving spouse was to be paid the "Net Income" from the Trust.

The consequences of these silent Trust documents meant that the investments in them were controlled by Default Rules- the Principal and Income Act and about 50% of the value of their Trusts would always be in bonds.[2] If either Robert or Jane died after the year 2005, without revising their current Credit Shelter Trust, the approximate (and unsatisfactory) end-values will be:

	VALUE OF THE TRUST [3] AFTER		
Start	**5 yrs.**	**10 yrs.**	**15 yrs**
$1,000,000	$1,201,000	$1,444,000	$1,736000

	20 yrs.	**25 yrs.**
	$2,087,000	$2,508,000

To Increase the End-Value of their Trust for Their Four Children, Robert and Jane Mathews had Changes Made in Their Credit Shelter Trusts.

Option 1: They gave investment directives to override the Default Rules. These directives increased the percentage of investments in good quality growth stocks to 100% from 50% (the amount designated by

(2) The Default Rule requires 50% in bonds. As the stocks increase in value, some stocks are sold and the proceeds again invested in bonds to maintain an approximate 50% in bond and 50% in stocks through out the life of the Trust.

(3) Every five years stocks were sold and bonds purchased to reestablish an approximate 50/50 % balance.

the Default Rule). By making this one change, Jane and
Robert Mathews expected that over the life of the Trust
the value of the stocks would at least increase at an
average rate of eight percent a year. Note: The past
history has been an increase of 12% so this expectation
could be considered conservative.

A financial directive to override the investment
"Default Rules" (50% in bonds/50% in stocks) is one
thing parents can do to increase the end-value of their
Trusts. There are other things that can be done also.

Option 2: The Mathews gave another new
directive regarding the payment of income from the
investments in their Trust. They replaced the current
directive in their Trusts that the "Net Income" which
was to be paid annually to the surviving spouse.
Instead they included a new directive requiring that
100% of the trustee fees and expenses are to be charged
to the income of the Trust.[4] If there are insufficient
funds from the income,[5] then any additional fees and

(4)   A grantor has the option of stating how the fees and
       expenses of their Trust are to be charged to their Trust.
       The grantor can state how all expenses and fees of the
       Trust are to be paid.

(5)   A $1 million Trust invested 100% in stocks, paying
       dividends of 0.9%, will yield a Gross Income in the first
       year of $9,000. This Gross Income would be expected to
       increase to about $12,000 in the fifth year and to about
       $18,000 in the tenth year. The job of the trustee or the
       investment manager selected by the trustee, under the new
       Uniform Prudent Investor Act, would be to invest in stock
       index funds and large mutual funds. Therefore, trustee fees
       of 0.75% or less can be negotiated.

expenses are to be charged to the principal of the Trust.[6]

If Option 1 and Option 2 are included, the value of the Trust,[7] over the Default Rules could be additionally increased to:

	Value, Default Rules	Value, With Options	Increase	
			Amount	%
5 Years	$ 1,201,000	$ 1,469,000	$ 268,000	22%
10 Years	1,444,000	2,158,000	714,000	49%
15 years	1,736,000	3,172,000	1,436,000	83%
20 years	2,087,000	4,660,000	2,573,000	123%
25 years	2,508,000	6,848,000	4,340,000	173%

Option 3: After exercising options 1 and 2, above, there is a third option that the Mathews can use to reduce the taxes on the surviving spouse's estate. This option states how the income of the Trust will be distributed.

The option is based on this concept: If the income is distributed to a spouse, who already has a large taxable estate, the money will then be added to the

(6)   Professional trustees will generally require this as a safety provision in the event the Gross Income does not fully cover expenses and fees.

(7)   Amounts were calculated by annual increasing the value of the stock by 8%. If the stocks increased at their annual historic rate of 12%, the value of the Trust would far exceed the amounts shown. The projections were made using Estate Planning Program Two described in Appendix H.

value of the estate could be taxed at a very high estate-tax rate when that surviving spouse dies. Or, if the surviving spouse has a large income from other sources and may not need all or part of the income from the Trust. In these cases, the trustee can give all or part of the income to the children, the spouse, or retain all or part of the income in the Trust.[8]

<u>"Safety Provision" for the Surviving Spouse</u>

As you consider the above financial directives in your Credit Shelter Trust that increase the end-value of the Trust for the children and other heirs, a Safety Provision for your surviving spouse deserves serious consideration.

Most Trusts have a general provision for the removing of funds from the principal of the Trust for the benefit of the surviving spouse. But this authority is at the sole discretion of the trustee. And, in the past, trustees have required extensive documentation before they agree to the payment of the requested funds. Other problems have also been encountered as indicated in Chapter 11.

To avoid delays or extensive proof of need, I recommend a "Safety Provision" that allows the surviving spouse to obtain additional funds if needed just by asking for them from the trustee. As discussed in Chapter 10, this power allows the surviving spouse to annually request from the trustee the greater of

(8)　　A legal term for this option when given to the trustee is "Sprinkling Powers."

$5,000 or 5% of the value of the Trust. And, within a stated number of days, the trustee must pay the amount requested.

Except for the immediate need of the surviving spouse, this power would not be expected to be used. If one of the children needed money, we recommend considering that the funds be available first from the Trust as determined and authorized by the surviving spouse as presented in Chapter 8.

Summary of your options

1. To increase the end-value of your Trust for the benefit of your children and other heirs, your Trust should give a directive requiring that all or a very high percentage of the funds in the Trust be invested in good quality growth stocks.

2. If your surviving spouse will have ample funds outside the Credit Shelter Trust, you might want to direct that all fees and expenses of the Trust are to be charged to the income. This will again increase the principal value of the Trust for your children and other heirs.

3. If your surviving spouse will have income needs mainly satisfied from other sources, consider providing for all or part of the income to be distributed to, or held in a separate Trust for the children, as well as giving the income to the surviving spouse. You can direct that these decisions can be made by the surviving spouse, not the trustee.

4. Finally, make sure your surviving spouse has a
safety net: the power to annually request up to
the greater of $5,000 or 5% of the value of the
Trust provides this safety.

WE WANT
THESE
SPECIFIC
OPTIONS
PUT INTO
OUR TRUST

Extra Money When It is Needed

<u>The $5,000 or 5% rule</u>

In addition to receiving an annual income from a Trust, there is another standard provision generally placed in the document.. It provides for additional funds for the lifetime income beneficiary (you, your spouse or another person). These additional funds are from the principal of the Trust and are released at the sole discretion of the trustee. This is another provision many grantors are not advised about.

This is the provision that allows the income beneficiary to annually request $5,000 or 5% of the value of the Trust (whichever is greater) without obtaining the approval of the trustee.[1] And, you can limit this provision to annual requests of only $5,000.

In this chapter we will:

1.   Explain the difficulties the surviving spouse has in receiving any extra money from the standard provision in most Trusts.

2.   Inform you of the work a trustee should do when following your wishes as expressed in the standard provision.

[1]   Internal Revenue Code Section 2041 entitled "Powers of Appointment," subsection (b)(2) which defines a general power of less than five (5%) percent or the greater of that and Five thousand ($5,000.00) dollars as not being a taxable lapse of a general power. Your attorney can advise you as to how these amounts are increased under the new tax law.

3.   Explain the legal liabilities a trustee can incur by granting the survivor's standard requests for funds without a proper investigation, documentation and reasons for doing so.

4.   Indicate how the grantor can give the surviving spouse access to extra funds on request.

A problem in Trusts

An example of the standard language in Trusts authorizing the payment of extra funds to the surviving spouse is that "The trustee is authorized to pay out of principal such sums necessary or proper for Income Beneficiary's health, maintenance, education, support, care, comfort, well being and general welfare."[2]

The requests for extra funds can be met with very different responses from trustees. The professional trustee may react in a way that the family member serving as trustee would not. But every trustee, whether a family member or a professional, is bound by the same laws, has the same liabilities for mismanagement.

The professional trustees, such as those in a bank or other professionals, has a knowledge of the law and experience in this area. The son, daughter, friend or

---

(2)   The above standard language can give the impression that due to its very broad authority the trustee can provide funds for almost any need of the Income Beneficiary. This may not be the case because the IRS has established requirements called "Ascertainable Standards." The standards are a test to determine the validity of any payments by the trustee if the Trust is to maintain its special tax status. Review this with your Trust attorney.

relative has limited experience and perhaps is a trustee in only this single instance.

Problems with "Trustee discretion"

The professional trustee is always concerned about balancing their responsibilities to the remaindermen (generally your children) and to the lifetime income beneficiary (generally your spouse). These professionals are equally concerned about the valid needs for these requests for funds as well as the possibility of lawsuits against the trustee by the remaindermen for actions that could be considered improper or that favored the income beneficiary.

Any request from the income beneficiary for funds from the principal of the Trust will of course result in the reduction in the value of the Trust. This in turn will reduce the future income from the Trust and the value the remaindermen will receive when the Trust is terminated.

Granting a request for even a relatively small amount, if removed from the principal of the Trust, will reduce the funds eventually given to the remaindermen. It can be argued that giving a total of just $50,000 of the principal of the Trust to you or your spouse by the trustee will reduce the funds the remaindermen could have received by $150,000 or more.

If there is an affirmative response to the request for funds, the trustee is responsible for complete and documented evaluation of the need for the funds according to the terms of the Trust, the law and court cases. If that is not done, the trustee has a potential future liability.

To guard against such future litigation from the remaindermen or claims by the IRS, the professional trustees not only determines the valid needs of the request, but also carefully and completely documents these requests. This is done to determine if the requested funds are necessary and proper according to the terms of the standard provision in a Trust for the income beneficiary's maintenance, education, support, care, comfort, well being and general welfare.

Professional trustees as part of this evaluation, determine if you or your spouse have funds from other sources, to meet your needs. And, the request for extra funds can be denied.

Professional trustees know they can be held financially liable for mismanagement or errors made in the handling of a Trust. The same applies to a family member or friend that you select to be your trustee. Professional trustees have years of experience in Trust management and they do it to the terms of the Trust and Trust law. Since the majority of Trusts do not give specific instructions on these types of issues, the professional management looks to the laws and court rulings on these loosely defined concepts found in most Trusts. And, generally the law does not favor the surviving spouse over the remaindermen.

Trustee must determine if request valid

A trustee has a duty, when the standard provision is in a Trust, to determine the valid need for extra funds requested by the Income Beneficiary. The trustee must fully document how they determined to grant or deny such requests. A trustee who has to justify why an action was taken several years before, without proper documentation, can find that future legal and financial liability may be the result.

Banks, after making their investigation, generally have various levels of approval required before the request is granted. A request for a small amount, in which there is a documented valid need, can be approved by one or more Trust officers. Requests for larger amounts, perhaps over $10,000 may go to a committee.

When an income beneficiary asks an experienced trustee for funds from the principal of the Trust, the experienced professional trustee will do the following:

1. Ask that the request be in writing and the reasons stated why these funds are requested.

2. Send a response asking the income beneficiary to provide:

   a. A complete financial statement.

   b. Copies of recent income tax returns and other information.

Solutions to this problem

As the grantor, your first solution is to provide from the Trust enough funds from the annual income so that you or your spouse are not continually placed in a position of needing extra funds from the Trust

Remember, the reason most individuals set up a
Credit Shelter Trust was to save up to $235,000 in
federal taxes. But, they did not do it to reduce the
annual income their surviving spouse would receive
from it.

To help ensure that you or your spouse have
a sufficient annual income from your Trust, consider
the recommendations in Chapter 7.

Anticipate probable needs

You can anticipate certain events that you
would expect to occur and have funds available from
the principal of the Trust for these purposes.

Examples: - A wedding in the family.
- The need for a new car.
- Special training or education for family
  members.
- Other specific needs that apply to your
  family and that you wish to take care of
  with funds from the Trust.

Do not let tax issues complicate family needs

Do not become overly concerned with tax
considerations that may complicate how smaller
amounts of extra funds are distributed. A general
recommendation is first to give the extra funds to the
surviving spouse. That person can determine how
these funds will be used. Chapter 8, covers how the
surviving spouse can make funds available to one or
more of your children, if that is your wish.

Strong family relationships

Remember that a strong continuing family relationship is one of your objectives. No one wants to place their surviving spouse in a position of saying to the children and grandchildren "wait until I die, then you will have lots of money." Since parents are living longer, you may want to provide for the needs of children in their middle years.

Receive extra funds just by asking

You have the right to state in your Trust that your spouse can receive up to $5,000 a year in additional funds just by asking for it. Your trustee is required to pay this amount within a certain time and without question. If you include these conditions, your trustee is required to do as you direct and is relieved of the responsibility for determining the validity and need of the requested funds. You or your spouse may then use these additional funds for any purpose.

In addition, you also have the right to state that your surviving spouse can receive a much greater amount - up to 5% of the value of the Trust.[3]

We do not recommend including the right to obtain 5% of the value of the Trust if you have provided for the Trust to pay a substantial annual income increased for inflation.

[3]   This is the maximum amount federal tax code and rulings allow the income beneficiary to annually withdraw from a Credit Shelter Trust. This amount is not cumulative. If the provision is not used in a prior year it cannot be added to the authority in the current year to remove 10% from the Trust. Your attorney can advise you on this.

If a Trust is currently paying a high annual income, say 5% of the value of the Trust and paying the Trust fees and expenses from principal, adding another 5% payout each year could result in a rapid decrease of the value of the Trust during periods of low interest rates on bonds and limited increases in the stock market.

In the above example, where a high annual income was required from the Trust, you could give the surviving spouse the power to annually obtain up to $5,000 from the Trust. You can withhold the power to remove 5% of the value of the Trust.

Avoid poor advice on trustee powers

One excuse for not doing the work we recommend is that "No one can plan out everything - so, let the trustee handle these problems when they come up." By now you know that this is not the best answer.

Few Trusts properly consider the needs of the surviving spouse in the later years. But you can project, with a strong degree of accuracy, what these needs might be. It can be anticipated that as the surviving spouse advances in age, medical needs increase. Nursing homes may eventually be required.

In many cases, family members no longer live in the same area. Sons, daughters and other family or friends can be hundreds of miles apart.

Provision should be considered in your Trust to pay the expenses for family members or friends who live at a distance to visit the surviving spouse in their later years to comfort them and ensure that they are receiving proper care.

A provision to make funds available for this contingency, when needed for these visits, can be placed into your Trust. Then, a son or a daughter could travel to visit the surviving parent regardless of how far away they lived. Grandchildren could also join in these visits.

This very important potential issue of the surviving spouse being in a nursing home should be considered. I recently visited with an older couple, living on the east coast. When discussing their plans, the wife mentioned that if required, she would move to a nursing home in that area familiar to her. But her two married daughters and grandchildren lived a great distance in Denver and in California. Resources for travel for both young families were limited.

The mother knew that the potential for either surviving spouse to become seriously ill or confined to a nursing home was real. It needed to be considered and funds provided from the Trust for these visits. A trustee is not required to pay these expenses unless this is clearly stated in your Trust

You must provide well-thought-out directives, otherwise the trustee is limited to the Default Rules. There are other instances where a grantor might believe the trustee will act, but the trustee may have no authority unless such is stated in the Trust.

Chapter 12

Trusts for a Second Marriage

A prenuptial agreement

Many second marriages include a prenuptial agreement. These agreements generally state that what each brings to the marriage will remain that person's property. These agreements are meant to protect the assets of each partner and to allow each individual upon their death to pass their assets directly to their own children and other heirs.

However, later in the marriage, very often the partner with the most assets wants to provide after his or her death the same standard of living for the surviving spouse. This requires a higher income than their spouse with the more limited assets can achieve. In such cases, Trusts[1] are often established to provide this higher income. A Marital Trust can be used along with a Credit Shelter Trust. The best way to learn how to do this is to study a few examples.

Both types of Trusts, mentioned above, allow a person to place assets, tax free at their death, in them. The Trusts will provide an income during the surviving spouse's lifetime. Who will receive the assets in the

---

(1) Insurance products could also be considered for part or all of the funds required. A life Insurance policy could be purchased on the life of the grantor and held in an Irrevocable Life Insurance Trust. The starting date of the annual payments to the recipient are unknown (the date depends upon the date of death of the grantor); the amount of annual payments to the recipient increases annually, for inflation; and the ending date for the annual payments (the date of death of the recipient) is also unknown. The excess funds, at the date of death of the recipient, are distributed to the heirs named by the grantor.

Trusts, after the death of the surviving spouse, is stated in the Trust document when it was signed by the grantor.

To provide for both the spouse and children

To properly establish such Trusts with appropriate options requires time to make reasonable projections that need to be clearly documented in the Trusts. If you plan to do this, tests should be made of these directives. They should include:

1). Projecting reasonable needs for the spouse you wish to provide for, and

2). Projecting the future value of your assets.

These kinds of Trusts also require frequent review. The review is to determine if the financial assumptions are still valid three or four years after they were established or last reviewed. Generally the financial assumptions were conservative, in order to ensure that adequate funds will be available to provide the income the surviving spouse will require. As a result, actual increases in the value of the estate can be greater than planned. When this occurs, it usually means that additional funds are available for the children with possible changes in the initial distribution of the grantor's estate. The following material includes examples of how to develop a plan and to test the assumptions upon which the plan has been prepared.

To the surprise of many grantors, the decision to provide for their surviving spouse is not in conflict with their wish to leave funds to their children. In most cases, a sizable amount of money can be given tax free to the children at the grantor's death, while funds to provide the needed income for the surviving spouse are held in Trust.

This is the advantage of proper estate planning. It is not the case that all of a person's estate must be held in Trust if there is the wish to provide for the surviving spouse of the second marriage. Many of the same principles apply here that were presented in Chapter 7 and in Appendix H - "How to Test Your Financial Directives."

The Starting Point

In most situations, the worksheets, Exhibits 1 and 2 - "Income Needs of Each Spouse' (see **Chapter 6**) are used as the starting point. Please note in these forms, all the income the surviving spouse receives from his or her resources is deducted from the annual amount that the spouse will need. Once an amount is determined as required from Trusts, the planning for how this will be accomplished starts. An example of this planning follows.

Second Marriages with assets of $800,000

In this example is a couple, Henry and Margaret Bright. Henry's first wife died and several years later he remarried. He is retired and receives an annual pension of $40,000. If Henry's first wife had survived him, she would have received half of Henry's pension. However, Henry's current wife - Margaret, if she survives him, will not receive any part of his pension.

At age 70, Henry has two grown children and Margaret, age 67, also has two grown children.

Henry owns, free and clear, the home they live in valued at about $125,000. He also has stocks currently worth about $ 600,000 and about $150,000 in CD's and bonds. His second wife, Margaret has CDs and bonds, in her own name valued at $250,000.

After carefully completing Exhibits 1 and 2, "Income Needs of Each Spouse", it was determined that Margaret would need, in 2001 dollars, $24,135 from Trusts Henry would establish. As part of the planning to determine the size of the Trust, an increase for the cost of inflation (estimated at three percent a year) was used.

The following table is a summary of the plan that was prepared based on the possibility that Margaret might live past age 100. Review in the table, column two, Margaret's ages and in column three the increasing amounts she will need.

Also look across to column six, the "Amount Required" to be placed in trust to provide the income payment to Margaret. The footnotes explain how these projections were made.

The actual calculation of the amount required to fund the Trust in each of the five-year periods was obtained by using Estate Planing Program One, down loaded from ccmtrust.com/the book.

			Amount to Fund Trust, if Henry Died		
Year	Margaret's Age	Trust Payment [1]	Year	At Age	Amount Required [2]
2001	67	$ 24,135	2000	70	$ 500,000
2003	70	26,373	2003	73	500,000
2008	75	30,574	2008	78	525,000
2013	80	35,444	2013	83	525,000
2018	85	41,089	2018	88	525,000
2023	90	47,633	2023	93	475,000
2028	95	55,220	2028	98	375,000

The Estate Plan

1. In 2001, the year the Trusts for Margaret were executed, Henry has a total estate valued at $875,000 including his home. His federal estate-tax exemption in 2001 is $675,000. According to the table above Henry needs $500,000 to provide the payments Margaret needs. In addition, the home should also be available for Margaret. So, Henry established a marital trust for Margaret with assets of $200,000. The Marital Trust

[1]   These amounts were obtained by increasing the annual income Margaret would need in 2001 by three percent for estimated annual cost of inflation.

[2]   The annual stock increase estimate was reduced from the historical 12% annual gain to 8% for the above projections. This was done to be conservative in estimating the funds required for Margaret from Henry's Trusts. If the 12% had been used, less funds would be required. The amounts required to fund the Trusts were developed by using Estate Planning Program One, that is available to you on the Internet. Appendix H indicates how the calculations can be performed to determine the amount of funding required for these types of Trusts.

included his home valued at $125,000 and $75,000 of his securities. Henry then used his $675,000 federal estate-tax exemption to: a). give directly at his death, tax free, $250,000 to his two children and b). hold the balance of $425,000 of his securities in a Credit Shelter Trust for Margaret's benefit.

The result is a total of $625,000 that would go into these Trusts for Margaret. Of this total amount, $500,000[3] would be in securities and $125,000 would be the value of his home.

2. Henry directed the following:

a. Trustee is to invest 50% of the funds in both Trusts in growth stocks and 50% in bonds, a conservative approach. If a greater percentage was invested in stocks, the funds required could be less.

b. Trustee is to pay directly the real estate taxes and insurance on his home and deduct these amounts from the funds Margaret is to receive each year. Henry further directs that if Margaret wants to move from their home, the trustee will sell it and purchase for Margaret a new residence of her choice with the proceeds.

c. Trustee is to pay Margaret an income of $24,135, if Henry died in 2001, the year the Trusts were executed. If he lived past 2001, he instructed the trustee to increase the $24,135 each year for inflation.

(3)   See Table on prior page

d.   Trustee is to pay the annual income to Margaret first from the income of the Marital Trust; and next from the income of the Credit Shelter Trust. Additional funds if required, would be taken first from the principal of the Marital Trust. This was done for estate-tax purposes.

Frequent review required for these types of Trusts

Henry intended two years later, in the year 2003, to review his financial position and his Trust documents. At that time he expected his stocks to grow in value from $600,000 to about $ 766,000.

Assuming no increase in value for his home, CDs, and bonds, Henry's total estate would then be worth $1,041,000 and his federal estate-tax exemption, in the year 2003, would be $700,000.

Henry planned to review the need for any changes first in his Trust provisions for Margaret.

1.   He believed that he had placed sufficient funds in the Trust he established for Margaret in the year 2000 (see table on page 116). This assumes that inflation had increased at 3% annually over the last three years. Henry would in the year 2003 redo Exhibit 1 "Income needs of Each Spouse" the results of which might require minor adjustments.

2.   If Henry's total assets in the year 2003 had grown from $875,000 to $1,041,000, he would also be able to increase the amount to be paid to his children, at his death. If no additional funds

were required in Margaret's Trust, Henry would be able to increase from $250,000 to $416,000 the amount his children would receive. And, this amount would be tax free.

The above planned changes are important reasons why estate planning documents need to be reviewed at regular intervals. In this case, Henry's assets were estimated in 2003 to increase $166,000, based on his estimate for his stocks. However, the value of the stocks could also have increased over $310,000 if the stocks grew at their historical rate. Or, the value of the stocks could have decreased.

No one can accurately project the exact amounts that will be available five or ten years from now. One can project the general results expected and have a plan to frequently update the projections.

Note: If the increases in securities values that Henry anticipated in the year 2003 occurred, they would allow him to consider the following changes:

1. He could increase the securities in the Trusts for Margaret from $450,000 to $575,000. The Total Value of the Trusts for Margaret, including the home, valued at $125,000 would be $700,000.

2. He could increase the amount given to his two children, at his death.

Henry also intended eight years later,[4] in the year 2008, to make a second special review of his

---

4) He still intended to review his Trust every 3 to 5 years for other potential changes.

financial position and his Trust documents. At that time:

He expected his stocks to have increased in value to about $1,125,000. If this occurred, Henry's total estate would then be worth $1,400,000 and his federal estate- tax exemption would be $1 million. Based upon the projections in the increase of the value of his estate, Henry planned to revise his Trusts to accommodate a changing financial position.

To increase the securities in the Trust for Margaret to $625,000. This would provide the maximum funds required. Henry would increase the amount that would go directly to his children to $650,000.

His documents would state that the remaining portion of his estate-tax exemption of $350,000 would be in stocks held in a Credit Shelter Trust. The balance of $400,000 would be held in a Marital Trust (of which $275,00 would be in securities and $125,000 would be the 2000 value of his home).

After the year 2008, when Henry would be 78 and Margaret age 75, Henry's assets could continue to grow. The first $350,000 of this growth would be given directly to his children tax-free, thereby using his full federal estate-tax exemption. After that, the taxes on his estate would then greatly increase. Henry would have several tax-saving techniques that he could then use. The most common type is a tax-free gift of $10,000 to each of his children. Charitable Remainder Unitrusts could also be established that would provide a lifetime income for them individually. And, outright gifts to churches and charities can be made.

Henry's potential changes in his Trust documents could be on an attached schedule. Then, only the attached schedule would be revised. This is an important drafting technique that Henry's attorney could use for these directives and certain other options, such as instructions for investing Trust assets.

However, it is important that an attorney be consulted when changes are to be made in an attached schedule.

You can provide for both the wife and the children

1. With proper planning, adequate provision can be made for both the wife of a second marriage and the husband's children from the first marriage.

2. But to do this a plan is required and should be completed before visiting an attorney.

3. Much smaller estates can also plan and obtain these benefits.

CHAPTER 13

Avoiding Future Tax Increases

The first basic Trust you establish is one that qualifies for your maximum federal estate-tax exemptions.

Avoiding state and local estate taxes

Depending upon the size of your estate and changes in the federal tax code, your next consideration is the avoidance of state and local government taxes. Taxes on your estate are of two general types. The first are taxes on your estate at your death. The second type are annual taxes on your estate as long as your assets are held in trust. Once your assets are distributed to your heirs, your heirs will then pay all future taxes on the earnings and the capital gains from these assets.

In most instances, the estate taxes that must be paid at death are normally determined by the state where the grantor has resided. Sometimes more than one state can make an estate-tax claim especially when a vacation home is located in another state.

With the exception of real estate, most of your assets can be placed in another location, outside of a state that levies a high taxes on a deceased grantor's estate. This is done by placing these assets in a state with very low or no estate taxes at death and avoiding the probate of these assets.

Many may argue that this cannot be done. Avoid using people who offer such advice. With a little planning you can do it.

And, after your death, your estate can continue to be managed in a state with low or no annual taxes on your Trust. This can happen even if your beneficiaries live in another state.

We must always keep in mind that governments need more income each year for their programs. And, while we may experience major estate-tax relief by the federal government, it is only temporary. A different administration can pass new laws that tax estates.

The solution is to establish Trusts that we hope will be "Grandfathered" to avoid any new estate-tax increases that in the future are passed into law. This may be difficult to do since changes in tax laws have been made that did not always grant grandfather status to prior contracts and agreements [1]

Taking advantage of any tax releif

It makes sense to draft estate-planning documents that take advantage of temporary estate-tax relief of the federal government while preserving former well-established positions as a fallback for protection against the future changes in federal estate taxes.

1) The worse case in recent years was the tax reform act in the nineteen eighties that removed the tax shelter for many real estate investments. Investors had entered into contracts requiring annual payments with the understanding that their tax shelter would offset the annual investment amount. But the change in the tax law in the eighties removed this particular tax shelter and did not grandfather prior legal agreements. The annual investment amounts still had to be made. This caused financial problems for many who had entered into these agreements.

It would be very foolish to build a plan for an estate worth many millions of dollars on the expectation that recent changes in the federal estate-tax law will last during the lifetime of the grantor - say thirty-five or forty years from now.

An example that needs to be expanded upon is the current practice of making reference to a section of the tax code rather than absolute amounts. Then as the absolute amounts change over the years in the tax code, the documents do not have to be rewritten.[2]

One concept is to place in documents language that states if future changes in the federal tax code remove, restrict or reduce any of the current federal estate-tax benefits, then the alternative provisions in the Trust would then apply.

An example of this would be a grantor who placed his entire estate, with a value say of $5 million in a tax-free Trust. This was done based on current laws that exempted this amount from federal taxation. But later the federal exemption was reduced to say $1 million and the concept of a Marital Trust[3] was restored in the federal tax code.

[2]   An example is the reference in estate-planning documents to the section in the IRS code on each individual's federal estate-tax exemption rather than the listing of amounts of estate-tax exemptions. The code lists the exemption amounts. The year the grantor dies determines the amount that is free of estate taxes and the amount that can be placed tax-free in a Credit Shelter Trust.

[3]   This is a Trust established for the benefit of a surviving spouse. See Chapter 14

Avoiding future tax increases

There is a price to pay in avoiding future tax increases., The grantor gives up the ability or options to make future changes. The first types of Trusts that may escape future changes in taxes and tax regulations will be irrevocable type Trusts.

Trusts such as Irrevocable Life Insurance Trusts, Charitable Remainder Unitrusts, Gift Trusts for the benefit of children in which the grantor is not the trustee and many others types of Trusts and contractual agreements have a common bond. Each of these Trusts is irrevocable and once established, the terms and conditions are generally locked-in.

Other types of Trusts such as Living Trusts that establish Credit Shelter and Marital Trusts will require careful drafting with fall-back alternatives in anticipation of revisions in the federal tax code. These Trusts are revocable and can be changed as tax laws change and the grantor is still alive and competent.

Once a grantor dies, these types of revocable Trusts become irrevocable.

Marital Trust Used with a Credit Shelter Trust

<u>What is a Marital Trust?</u>

In addition to your state and federal estate-tax exemption, the assets you leave to your surviving spouse pass tax free to that person provided they are a United States citizen.

It is not necessary that your surviving spouse has control of these assets to qualify for the tax-free status upon your death. You can place some or all of these additional assets into a Marital Trust for the survivor.

You then can exercise great control over these assets. There is a requirement that all the income from this type of Trust be paid to your surviving spouse.

The interest and dividend income paid from a Marital Trust is taxed at the spouse's regular income-tax rates. Any distributions of the original principal from the funds placed in the Marital Trust are not taxed since these are funds your surviving spouse could have received, tax free at the grantor's death. When your surviving spouse dies, the value of the Marital Trust is added to the surviving spouse's estate and is subject to regular estate taxes.

The grantor of the Marital Trust controls who is to receive these assets at the death of the survivor, less any estate taxes, by stating in the document the names of the Remaindermen. Marital Trusts, combined with Credit Shelter Trusts are used in many second marriage situations as discussed in Chapter 12.

Marital Trusts and Credit Shelter Trusts are also used when the Grantor believes that the surviving spouse is not capable of or interested in managing these funds.

Sometimes a grantor establishes a Marital Trust to avoid undue influence by others to obtain funds from the surviving spouse.

<u>Use a Marital Trust to increase</u>
<u>value of the Credit Shelter Trust</u>

A Marital Trust can provide the income your surviving spouse will need, while allowing your Credit Shelter Trust to greatly increase in value for your children and other heirs.

A grantor can increase the value of a Credit Shelter Trust for the children by using the techniques in Chapter 10. To do this, the grantor might give a directive that 100% of the assets are to be invested in good quality growth stocks and that all of the fees and expenses of the Trust are to be charged to the income of the Trust.

If the above is done, the surviving spouse will receive a very low income from the Credit Shelter Trust. The income needs of the surviving spouse are then paid from the Marital Trust. In many cases, the actual income paid from the investments will not be sufficient. To compensate for this, instructions are given in the Trust to invade the principal for the additional funds required.

Be aware of Key Options

When a grantor leaves both a Credit Shelter Trust and a Marital Trust for the support of his surviving spouse, special instructions are required in each trust in order to have the Credit Shelter Trust grow in value for your children and other heirs.

Remember the Marital Trust after the death of the surviving spouse, may be subject to high estate taxes rates. The Credit Shelter Trust contains the tax-exempt funds.

A goal should be that all of the needs of your surviving spouse should come first from the Martial Trust. The invasion of principal article in the Credit Shelter Trust should state:

" No funds from the principal of this Trust can be paid to my surviving spouse until the funds in the Marital Trust are depleted."

High Value Estates

When the assets of a person are of great value, other estate planning techniques should be considered during the lifetime of both the husband and the wife. You will find several of these alternatives in this book.

People with a substantial net worth, whether they are single or married, should seek extensive advice on these various estate planning alternatives. They should develop a complete plan for their estate and give careful consideration to available options.

Safeguards for the Assets in Your Trust

<u>Avoid Boilerplate Provisions</u>

A major portion of family assets are placed in Trust. But the boilerplate provisions in most Trusts do not provide any safeguards for these assets.

The traditional boilerplate provisions state that 1). no bond will be required by the trustee and 2). the trustee will not be responsible to any court for reporting their actions.

Added to the above are Default Rules which will allow a trustee to write a sizeable check on the assets of the Trust for deposit to the trustee's personal account without being questioned by the bank.

For reasons presented here, I recommend that the Trust should state that all funds and securities in the Trust are to be held by an appropriate custodian or at least be held in a brokerage account. And, that copies of the custodian or brokerage statements be sent to all beneficiaries of the Trust.

The following are some of the administrative duties of a trustee that a custodian or brokerage firms will do for a small fee or no charge.

1.   Take physical possession of the funds and securities.

2.   Notify all appropriate parties and organizations that as trustee you hold the stocks, bonds, notes, etc. and that payments, reports, etc. are to be made to the trustee.

3.   Collect all funds, dividends, interest, etc. and immediately deposit these funds in a money market account or similar account to earn short term interest until the funds are paid to the income beneficiary or to be used for other authorized payments or investments.

4.   Provide a detailed copy of a transaction ledger to all the beneficiaries of the Trust at least quarterly if not monthly. [1]

5.   Provide to all the beneficiaries of the Trust a statement listing in detail all of the funds and securities in the Trust with their current market value at least quarterly if not monthly. [1]

6.   Prepare reports of each year's complete activity in the account for the preparation of annual state and federal fiduciary tax returns.

7.   Annually send the income beneficiaries a statement of their taxable earnings and tax payment withheld. Send copies to the state and federal government.

Why would any family member or friend, serving as your trustee, want to do the above work when the Trust departments of many banks will be the custodian

[1]   Unless your clearly state these requirements in your Trust, your trustee is not required to give to your beneficiaries periodic statements on the value of the Trust, and the types of securities and other assets held in the Trusts. Your trustee may assume that you do not want them to have this information since the requirement to provide it is not in your Trust.

and do this work for a reasonable fee? At the very minimum, a brokerage house will hold the cash and securities in an account for no fee.

One respected bank in our city charges one-tenth of one percent a year to be the custodian. They do have a minimum fee of $800 a year as custodian. In your Trust give the ability to your trustee to change custodians. This will allow the trustee to change banks if the current one decides to greatly increase their custodial fees.

Stockbrokers will also serve as custodians and a fee may be charged. For no fee, brokerage firms may handle the funds and securities in an account at their local offices. This no-fee account will provide the first six required duties of a trustee listed above.

Brokerage firms, at the local branch will do this work, without a fee, based on their expectation that when securities are bought or sold the transaction will be done through their firm.

If you select either a bank or a stock brokerage firm, they may require a copy of your Trust for review by their legal department.

A family member, as trustee, can hire a CPA who will prepare and file the annual state and federal fiduciary tax returns. The CPA will also prepare and file the required taxable income forms.

You may have heard of someone who as a trustee invaded the funds entrusted to them and used them for their own personal projects. These cases often start with the person just "borrowing" the funds for a short time with the expectation of repaying it at a later date.

Such things can easily occur when the document does not contain any safeguards, such as having a custodian and requiring frequent reports to all of the heirs. Most state statutes are broadly written, they do not provide any safeguards for the assets in the Trust if it contains the typical boilerplate "that the trustee is not responsible to any court" This is one of the reasons why we recommend directives be placed in the Trust requiring that a custodian or a third party (such as a brokerage house account) is required to handle the assets for the Trust and to send reports to all the beneficiaries as well as the trustee.

Family problems result when monthly or quarterly reports on the status of the Trust are not given to all the beneficiaries.

I have heard may complaints from family members. When a sister asked her brother, who was the trustee, for a written report on the value of the Trust, he responded, "Don't you trust me, everything is fine." In most cases, the records of a family member or friend serving as trustee are not properly maintained - so, supplying reports would be difficult.

<u>Use a custodian</u>

Use of a custodian or a qualified third party and the frequent reports they will send to keep all the beneficiaries informed will avoid suspicions and family alienations. These can develop when there is no regular accountability for all to read.

You can start with your broker

You can state in your document that your account with (your current broker and his company or your bank as custodian) is to be maintained by them and that all marketable securities and cash are to be held in this account.

You can state that this bank or brokerage firm will send, at least quarterly, a report on all the activities within the account (Trust account) and the current market value of all securities to all beneficiaries

You can state that your trustee and successor trustees can remove and replace the bank, brokerage or qualified third party by giving notice of their removal. And, that all transfers of funds and securities are to be made between the bank or brokerage firm terminated and to the newly designated bank or brokerage.

Why would any trustee want to do the work a Trust custodian or qualified third party will do? Why would a grantor leave this simple safeguard procedure out of a Trust?

If a potential trustee were to object to the above provisions, consider appointing another person as your trustee.

The statements that all custodians or brokerage houses send out is a complete audit trail. It lists every transaction that has taken place. If a dividend check is received on the 15th, the report indicates who it was from, and the amount, and when this dividend was deposited into the money market account.

If income or principal payments are made to the surviving spouse or other income beneficiaries, the report indicates the amount paid, the date and the name of the person receiving these funds.

If securities are purchased or sold, the report indicates the date, names of the securities and the cost or proceeds. If a lawyer or CPA is paid for work done for the Trust, the date, amounts paid and the name of the attorney or CPA is given.

At the end, the report gives the market value of all securities held and cash or money fund balances.

This is the type of report that should be sent to all of the beneficiaries. It will also be of great help to your trustee and will greatly reduce your trustee's administrative work. At year end, a statement is sent summarizing all of the taxable events that year. This statement can be given to the CPA who will prepare the annual federal and state fiduciary tax returns and the required state and federal forms of income payments from the Trust.

Living Trusts to Avoid Probate

Your Primary document

Grantors of Trusts have many options. A very important one is the use of a Living Trust as your estate planning document. This entire chapter will be devoted to that subject. I've done this because many people start their estate planning with the establishment of a Living Trust into which is placed their Credit Shelter Trust, and perhaps a Marital Trust. Yet for many, this was done without any consideration of their many important options presented in the preceding chapters.

They selected the Living Trust since it would avoid probate. For many, it was the only reason influenced, no doubt, by the numerous presentations made on the benefits of this type of estate planning document. This method of settling for a Trust based on tax considerations only, falls short in many ways.

It is only after you have developed a specific plan and know what you want to do that the proper type of estate planning document can be selected. Without a plan, the selection of a Living Trust will only provide the benefits of avoiding probate and perhaps saving about $235,000 in federal estate taxes, if both the husband and wife have a Living Trust prepared.

Assets that remain in your name will still go through the probate process. And, if the husband and wife have not divided their assets properly, the federal estate-tax saving is reduced and may not even exist. Much of what a Living Trust does not do, unless specific directives are added to these boilerplate forms, is completely unknown to many who have them.

Living Trusts do not avoid estate taxes

A few may be confused and attribute another benefit to a Living Trust such as avoiding federal estate taxes. They are not correct in this assumption either.

If properly prepared and funded, Living Trusts can combine a married couple's individual federal estate- tax credit for a combined estate-tax saving that will double the amount an individual has.[1] But this can also happen with properly prepared Credit Shelter Trusts placed in Wills.

Of course tax savings are important. But, you do not have to accept all the limitations contained in the rest of these form documents. Use the tax advantage part, but do not relinquish the many other options you have and can give directives for in your document.

Default Rules control Living Trusts but you can override them

Whatever type of Trusts are established in your Living Trust, the state Default Rules will control them. But you can use the options presented in this book to override these rules. For instance, your surviving spouse will still receive the same low income discussed in Chapter 7 unless in your Living Trust you use the options presented in that chapter.

---

(1)   In 2001 each individual has a federal estate-tax exemption of \$675,000. A married couple in their Living Trusts or Wills can combine their individual exemptions to give \$ 1,350,000 to their children and other heirs.

Unless you consider each one of the more than twenty major options, summarized in the check list starting on page 159 and place those you want in your Living Trust, not one of them will be available to provide for and to protect your family.

What is a Living Trust

A Living Trust, sometimes called a Loving Trust,[sm] is a revocable[2] Trust and is prepared to protect your estate from probate. You do not save one cent of estate taxes over a Credit Shelter Trust or other options available to you in a Will.. Avoiding probate is accomplished by changing the title of assets to the name of the Living Trust. Each asset's title must be properly changed to the name of the Trust in order to avoid probate for that asset. However, your ownership and all your rights to those assets in your Living Trust will not change.

An example would be if you own many different stocks and bonds and want to put them into your Living Trust. When this transfer is completed the securities will avoid the probate process. One way to accomplish this is if these securities are in your account at a brokerage house, notify the brokerage house to change the title of your account to the name of your Trust. This is the only act required, you must be absolutely sure it is done. When it is, your following monthly statements should reflect this change. The statement itself will be in the title of your Living Trust.

---

(2)   A Trust in which the Grantor reserves the right to revoke the entire document; withdraw any property transferred to the Trust, or change any or all of the terms of the Trust.

Nothing else changes. You still have all the rights you had when the account was in your name. If you have check-writing privileges and a credit card with your brokerage account, you can still have them or obtain them. There is no tax event caused by the title change. The interest, dividends and capital gains are still reported to you each year and as usual, go on your tax return. The only important difference is that the title of your account has changed

You continue to call your broker with your instructions when you want to buy or sell a security or have a check sent to you. The checks you write on your account or the credit card purchases you make are still signed by you. However, you sign as your trustee. Nothing else you do is different.

If you want to remove some or all of the securities from your Living Trust, you can do so. If you want to make changes in any part of your Living Trust or even cancel it, you can do so.

You must properly transfer each asset you own to the Living Trust if you do not want it to go through probate. Avoiding probate is the major reason for establishing a Living Trust. Any statements that might lead you to presume that a Living Trust avoids estate taxes are not true.

Before a married person transfers any assets to their Living Trust, that person should have an overall plan as to how the value of the assets fit into the combined estate-tax exemptions of both parties in the marriage.

Assets a married couple own that are held jointly with right of survivorship (such as their home) pass to the surviving spouse without going through probate. If your want to include your part of the property in your Living Trust, a change in title is required.

Other assets you own that name a beneficiary such as life insurance, IRAs and other retirement accounts do not go through probate.

Living Trust Problems

Living Trusts can also present many problems. A major one is that the very broad powers given to the grantor during his or her lifetime are not reduced and restricted after the grantor's death. Usually there is no provision in the Trust to do this once the grantor has died.

In Living Trusts the grantor's emphasis is on having the fullest range of powers to act while he or she is alive. As an example, authority is given to the grantor to:

1.   Hold securities of any type in the Living Trust.

2.   Buy, sell and trade in securities of any nature, including short sales, and on margin.

3.   Buy, sell and trade in commodities, commodity futures contracts and options on commodity future contracts.

4.   Buy, sell, trade or deal in precious metals of any kind.

Most grantors of a Living Trust do not use these very broad powers to engage in high risk investments. But they are there if ever the grantor wanted to use them. The problem is that they continue to exist even in the event the grantor becomes incapacitated or dies. As a result, these powers are passed to the successor trustee. If this trustee is inexperienced in Trust work and not properly guided, they may believe that the grantor intended them to use these powers to engage in high risk investments.

The same problem exists with Trusts established in your Will. These Trusts, both in your Will or in your Living Trust, generally indicate that they are to be governed by the state statutes which we have referred to and discussed several times. These statutes give very wide authority to the trustee. An important thing to remember is that these wide-ranging powers in the state statutes can be controlled and restricted by the grantor if he gives proper directives in the document.

A "Living Trust" is a "Revocable Trust."

After you establish this Revocable Trust called a Living Trust, anything you put into it you can remove at a later date. You lose no control over the assets. You are the grantor; the trustee; and the beneficiary of the Trust. Your tax identification number does not change. It is your Social Security number and remains so.

After your attorney prepares your Revocable Living Trust, make sure the assets you want to include in it are actually put in it. In many cases, a grantor established a "Living Trust" and initially funded it with $10.00 in the attorney's office but then neglected to add any other assets. As a result, everything not included in the Living Trust went through probate.

You add such assets to your Revocable Trust by having the title to each of them changed or having a listing of the items attached to and made part of the Trust. For real estate titles, your attorney can have the records changed to place their title in the name of the Trust. This is especially important and saves time and expense for property that may be located in another state.

After your death, many issues in your Living trust will be controlled by the Default Rules of your state just the same as they control the Credit Shelter Trust created in your Will.

There is basically only one benefit from a Living Trust. You escape probate for the assets you actually placed in it If you own property in another state, you can avoid going through a second probate in that state.[3]

A Living Trust contains provisions found in other estate planning documents. One provides for another person to act for you as a successor trustee of your Living Trust when you are unable to do so. This power only relates to those assets that are in your Living Trust. It is not a replacement for a Durable Power of Attorney that will apply to assets that are not in the Living Trust. This is an important distinction.

Prior to having a Living Trust or any other type of Trust prepared, you first need to carefully plan what you want to have happen with your estate.

Unfortunately, many people do not do this. As a result their Living Trust, and other estate planning documents are carefully secured in safe deposit boxes, along with all the errors and omissions that render them deficient and inadequate.

WE FOUGHT FOR
YOUR FREEDOM !

USE THIS FREEDOM
IN YOUR TRUST
DOCUMENTS TO
PROTECT YOUR FAMILY

Durable Powers of Attorney,
Pour-Over-Wills
and Medical Directives

Your basic set of documents

All of your basic set of estate planning documents are revocable. The term revocable means that the grantor can change, modify or cancel these basic documents at any time

Will or Pour-Over-Will

As a minimum you should have a Will. A Will appoints an executor of your estate and successor executors if the initial person so named is unable to serve. It states how your assets are to be distributed and, if there are beneficiaries who are minors, it names trustees or guardians of the funds for those minors. A Will may name the trustee and successor trustees for any special Trust you established such as a Credit Shelter Trust and a Marital Trust. A grantor's rights, financial and management options to consider for inclusion in a Will are contained in the prior chapters.

If you have a Living Trust, a Pour-Over-Will is also prepared since there are generally some assets still remaining in your name that are not in the Trust. Though you may think that you have all of your assets in your Living Trust, a Pour-Over-Will provides protection in the event that such is not the case.

Both the Will and the Pour-Over-Will go through the probate process.

Durable General Power of Attorney

A Durable General Power of Attorney is an important document. It gives the person whom you designate as your agent very broad powers to act for you during your lifetime should you become disabled or incompetent. In these circumstances, the person you designate has the power to mortgage, sell or otherwise dispose of any real or personal property without advance notice to you or approval by you.

Each state has statutes that authorize and fully describe powers granted in this document. Since a Durable General Power of Attorney has such broad powers, it must be properly prepared, witnessed and notarized.

A Durable General Power of Attorney usually does not authorize anyone to make medical or other health care decisions for you. If you want this done, you must sign a Health Care Power of Attorney, discussed below.

Health care power of attorney

The Health Care Power of Attorney is also an important legal document. You should be aware that it gives the person whom you designate as your agent very broad powers to make health care decisions for you when you are no longer capable of doing that for yourself.

The person named must act consistently with your desires, as sometimes stated in the document, or as otherwise known to them. Unless you state otherwise, the person named has the same authority to make decisions about your health care as you would have done.

The person you appoint should be someone you know and trust. You should discuss this document with them. You have the right to revoke the authority given in the document. You do so by notifying the person you selected as your agent of this change or notifying your attending physician, the hospital, or other heath care provider, either orally or in writing of the revocation.

<u>Document must be accessible</u>

1. The person(s) you have selected as your agent may need this document immediately in case of an emergency that requires a decision concerning your health care. You should keep the document where it is immediately available to those you have named. One solution is to give each person selected an executed copy of it. You may also want to give an executed copy of this agreement to your physician. Some people keep a copy in the glove compartment of their car when they travel.

2. If you are married and your spouse has established a Trust for you, consider including instructions in the Trust to pay the expenses of the person(s) you have selected for the responsibility of Health Care Power of Attorney. Generally a son or daughter is chosen as your agent. Years later, they may live hundreds of miles away. They could incur substantial travel and living expenses while making sure you have

the best care. As your agent, they have access to your records; can obtain the opinions of other specialists and, if required, have you moved to a major hospital in another city for treatment. They should be with you at such a critical time. The payment of their expenses necessary to carry out this responsibility should be in a Trust or other documents.

Living Will

A Living Will is another important document to consider. Most states have recently passed legislation that supports a person's right to determine if extraordinary means should be used to maintain their life or if they wish a natural death. It addresses the issues of an incurable or irreversible mental or physical condition with no reasonable expectation of recovery.

The conditions for its use are if:

1.   You are in a terminal condition.

2.   You are permanently unconscious, or

3.   You are conscious but have irreversible brain damage and will never regain the ability to make a decision and express your wishes.

Removing Assets From Your Estate to Reduce Estate Taxes

The many methods

There are many ways that you can give assets to your children and others to reduce your state and federal estate taxes. Most are simple. Others may be a little complicated and must be done properly if they are to be allowed by the taxing authorities.

Should you consider removing assets from your estate? To determine your need to do so, first list the items you own and the estimated current market value of each. Next, make a reasonable estimate of their future values five and ten years from now.

When this is completed, compare the total value of your assets to the federal and state estate-tax laws. If the value of your estate, either now or in the foreseeable future, is over your exemption or require the payment of capital gains taxes after your death, you may want to consider removing assets from your estate.

If you want to reduce your estate taxes, there are a number of things you can consider. The methods presented in this chapter are those most commonly used. There are other techniques, some more complex. If you have a sizeable estate, you should consult frequently with a tax attorney. New tax laws and recent tax court rulings may indicate a need for you to consider new tax-saving actions.

Removing Your Home from Your Estate:
A Qualified Personal Residence Trust.

The permanent residence and perhaps a vacation home represent a significant portion of most estates. Removing all or part of them from your estate can substantially reduce the taxes that must be paid at your death. Yet during your lifetime, you can continue to live in these places and transfer ownership at a discounted amount.

A helpful example is John and Mary Mahoney who own a home with a current market value of $200,000. They also own a vacation home, valued at $100,000. Both properties are in their names as joint owners with right of survivorship. This means that whoever dies first, the surviving spouse will own the two properties outright. There will be no estate tax at the death of the first partner. When the second spouse dies, both homes will be subject to an estate tax at what is then the current market values.

The Mahoneys decided that they want to remove both properties from their estate. To do this, they will transfer ownership to their children. If, however they make the transfer this year, they must use the current market value of each of their two properties. This is $300,000 and will reduce their lifetime federal estate-tax exemption by that amount. Such a high and unnecessary reduction can and should be avoided and there are ways to accomplish this.

A method the Mahoneys can use to remove the homes from their estate is to deed their homes into Trusts for their children. The value used for gift tax purposes could then be as low as about $100,000. The Mahoneys could also continue to live in their home and use their vacation property during the period of the

Trust, say ten or twelve years. Any increase in value of the current $300,000 will be out of their estate assuming the grantors survive the term of the Trusts.

If they wish to remain in their home past the period of the Trust, they can make an agreement, at the time the Trust is executed, to pay rent to the children and continue to live there.

There is a potential problem. If either Mr. Mahoney or Mrs. Mahoney dies before the ending date of their individual Trust, that spouse's share of the homes will be included in their estate, as it would have been if their Residence Trust had never been established. Therefore, you need to select a reasonable time period for both the husband's Trust and the wife's Trust. This time period would be based on the ages and life expectancy of each spouse when the Trusts are established.

Using Life Insurance: Irrevocable Life Insurance Trust

You can set up an Irrevocable Life Insurance Trust to accept policies on your life and remove the proceeds from your estate. If this is not done and the husband has life insurance policies, the wife, who is generally the income beneficiary, will receive an additional annual income and other benefits. And, at the wife's death the children will receive the proceeds tax free.

When the surviving spouse dies, taxes will be due on that estate if it exceeds his or her exemption. For a married couple, this is what estate planning is about -

reducing state and federal taxes on estates after the second partner dies. This is accomplished by using the tax exemption on the estate of the first partner to die by deliberately avoiding the full use of the Marital Deduction.

If the wife were to die first, and the children were the contingent beneficiaries, the proceeds of the husband's life insurance would be added to his estate and would be subject to state and federal estate taxes.

To avoid this high taxation, the first thing to consider is transferring your current life insurance to an Irrevocable Life Insurance Trust. You must live for at least three years after the date of the transfer for the death benefits under existing policies to be excluded from your taxable estate.

Once you have established this Irrevocable Life Insurance Trust, additional life insurance can be purchased by the Trust. If the Trust purchases the policy there is no three-year waiting period for the death benefits to be excluded from your taxable estate.

The Irrevocable Life Insurance Trust must be the owner and beneficiary of your policies. The Trust would then provide for your spouse, children and other heirs according to the directives you place in it.

Always use an attorney to establish an Irrevocable Life Insurance Trust. Until the Trust has been finalized, do not purchase additional life insurance. When the Trust is completed, the Trust should purchase this new coverage with funds you give the trustee. This avoids the three-year exclusion period

Annual Tax-Free Gifts

Another method frequently used to reduce estate taxes is annual tax-free gifts. You and your spouse each can give $10,000, tax free, to as many people as you choose. If you have three children, together you can give $60,000, tax free, to them each year, $120,000 if they are married, since you can also give gifts to their spouses. If you have grandchildren, each of you can give $10,000 to each of them every year (a total of $20,000 to each grandchild).

Consider a Gift Trust for young children

This type of Trust avoids many of the problems associated with the Uniform Transfer to Minor Act (UTMA). Funds can be held as long as the grantor wants from the children past ages 18 or 21. The Trust directives determines how the funds will be used for education and other needs. A minor problem is that the parent can not be the trustee. But a relative, friend, etc, can. The parent can be the "Trust Protector" to oversee what is happening, and replace the trustee if needed.

Gifts Greater than $ 10,000
You can make gifts greater than $10,000. But most gifts currently over $10,000 will reduce your $675,000 life-time estate-tax exemptions.

Gifts over $10,000 that will not reduce your estate-tax exemptions

There are certain types of gifts that can be given above the $10,000 that will not reduce your estate- tax exemptions. These include payments you make directly to schools for tuition and directly to the doctors and hospitals for the medical care of your children, grandchildren and others.

For most individuals this is a better alternative than placing funds into a Uniform Transfer to Minor Act account (UTMA). There is the dangerous possibility that at 18, the child can take the UTMA funds and do whatever they like. To avoid the risk, you hold the funds and you can say "I'll pay for your college education." And, you can add, "I'll buy you a car if your grades are good and you are on the Dean's list."

Checks you write directly to the school for that child are not included in your current $10,000 annual gift limit. And, they do not reduce your estate-tax exemption.

Charitable Remainder Unitrusts

Other alternatives are Charitable Remainder Unitrusts. People leave money to churches, charities and other qualifying tax-exempt organizations in their Wills.

Often grantors are not aware that they can establish a Charitable Remainder Unitrust and receive a high income from it for the remainder of their life. If they establish such a Trust they can also designate that after their own death, a second person can continue to receive the income during their lifetime

This type of Trust has many advantages such as a tax credit in the year the Trust was established and this can greatly increase your income from these assets

Increasing Your Annual Income

If you have assets that have greatly appreciated in value and now yield little or no annual income, you can obtain your first benefit by placing those assets in this type of Trust. These assets may include a home, other real estate, stocks, or a valuable collection, etc.

As an example, if you give to the Trust an asset worth $100,000, you can receive a tax credit of perhaps $45,000. In addition you can now also receive an annual income of say 7% or 8% of the value of your gift.

Family Limited Partnership

A Family Limited Partnership is another method that allows you to transfer to your children, each year, shares of limited partner ownership while you still maintain full control. This may be stocks, real estate, a business, or almost anything of value. This is the only technique where you can retain all the power of an owner, but not be taxed as an owner.

When a Family Limited Partnership is established, you and perhaps your wife become the general partners. Based on the fair market value of the assets in the partnership, you give limited partnership shares annually, valued at $10,000 or less, tax free to each child.

Limited partners have no say in the management of the asset or profits paid out each year. You can give away 99% as Limited Partnership interests over the years and still maintain control as the general partners. Sometimes the general partner is a corporation for the protection of the general partner.

If the assets in a Family Limited Partnership increase in value, then each annual gift of the $10,000 Limited Partnership shares will greatly increase in value in future years.

Family Limited Partnerships that hold listed securities are easier to evaluate annually compared to partnerships holding real estate. And since there is no market for these Limited Partnership interests, the value of the gift can be discounted

Family Limited Partnerships, Life Insurance Trusts, Buy/Sell Agreements, etc. should only be done with good professional advice. Using these methods to reduce estate taxes, without a competent professional's advice, can later present severe problems with the tax authorities. If this happens, the goals and benefits you hoped to receive will be greatly reduced and even eliminated.

Include Your Children if Possible, in New Business Ventures

Including your children and your other heirs in a new business venture can have many benefits. A good example that incorporated this idea was the purchase of an operating business

The business had substantial real estate and equipment. Mortgages and other loans were to be used in the purchase of the equipment. The buyer was advised to purchase the assets of the business, not the stock.

All of the real estate and equipment was placed into a limited partnership. The operating company (sales income, inventory and payroll expense, accounts receivable and payable, etc.) was in a corporation.

In the limited partnership, the children were made limited partners for 90% of the value of the partnership, the parent (the buyer) became a 10% general partner. The total value of the limited partnership was over $ 4 million. But the debts placed on these assets was very high. Therefore, the $10,000 annual gift covered the cost of each child's share of their limited partnership interest.

The operating company, the corporation, leased the real estate and operating equipment from the partnership. The lease payments covered the debt payments and other expenses such as real estate taxes. Most of the profits of the partnership were sheltered by depreciation taken on the real estate and the equipment.

It was estimated that after ten years, the debt on the property would be reduced by over 60%. And, the real estate, initially purchased at about $ 3 million, would increase in value by at least $ 1 million (a part of this increase would be caused by inflation).

When the above happened, the original debts of the limited partnership were reduced from about $ 4 million to $ 1.6 million (increasing the value of the limited partnership by $2.4 million). This coupled with the estimated ten-year increase in the value of the real estate of $1 million yielded an equity in the limited partnership of $3.4 million.

As 90% limited partners, the children's share, was $ 3 million. Even after a capital gains tax, the children's share as a result of this planning would be substantial. Each of the children's share was in a Trust, prepared by an attorney. The Trust stated that only the income would be paid to the child starting at age 21. A third of the principal was to be paid to each child when they reached the ages of 25, 35 and 45.

In this situation the parent had definite control of the limited partnership. He could use the assets for other business ventures and not distribute them to his children and, as general partner, he could place new mortgages on the assets and have the tax-free use of several millions of dollars.

Check List for Your Family's Needs

Complete before visiting an attorney

Attached is a check list of items for you to consider prior to visiting your attorney. The items on this list are key grantor options that need to be considered. These are the options we presented in this book. Additional references to them can be located in the index.

The answers of husbands and wives may differ on this check list. If married, make a copy for each partner.

Attorney consultation without charge

Once you have completed this check list, make copies of it. Then arrange for a consultant with a Trust attorney. Most of them will meet with a prospective client for 45 minutes or an hour without charge. Bring with you the extra copy you have made of the completed check list because it is during this initial meeting that you will cover the scope of work you want accomplished.

Have ready to present and discuss items on your check list, your list of assets[1] and the names of family members.

---

(1)   If you want to review and use forms to assist you in listing your assets, and other key items, go to our web site, www.ccmtrust.com and download the forms available there.

Select your attorney with care

You may have to interview several attorneys before selecting the one who will best serve your needs and do so at a reasonable expense.

The work you require should be done by an attorney who is trained in and whose practice is in estate taxes. The work you will require is not normally performed by an attorney in general practice.

Board certification of an attorney as a specialist in estate planning is not by itself justification for selecting an attorney to handle your estate planning needs. At this time, these certifications are given to many attorneys. Some have not been evaluated or tested on their knowledge and ability to know and understand the options every grantor should consider and that are on our check list.

For estate plans many attorneys use preprinted form documents. Many Trust attorneys have modified these forms and have added a few additional articles for items they like to include in the documents they prepare. Very few attorneys have prepared or include articles to cover the important financial and management options you have and that are covered in our check list.

However, with a bit of perseverance you will find a good Trust attorney who will consider, in a positive way, your objectives. It will require that the attorney create new articles to accomplish your objectives. And, this work will greatly add to his knowledge as a Trust attorney and to yours as a grantor.

NOTE: Under the last column entitled "Include" indicate by a check mark if you want this option in your documents. An asterisk (*) next to an option number indicates that I recommend including it.

OPTIONS FOR:

A. My Spouse's Income:

Option	Description	Include
1.*	Annual Income to be paid to my surviving spouse: Starting amount this year $ _____ Increased for inflation	

2. *	My spouse has complete authority to obtain an additional $5,000 each year from the trust.	

3. *	Additional funds required from the trust will be paid at sole discretion of my trustee.	

B. My Spouse is to be the head of the Family

Option	Description	Include
4.*	My spouse can instruct my trustee to distribute income to my children.	

5. *	My spouse can instruct my trustee to distribute principal to my children	

6. *	To protect my spouse from excessive distributions from principal, I establish amounts below which distributions can not be made.	

B. My Spouse to be the head of the Family (continued)

Option	Description	Include
7. A	When distributions of income are made, they are to be made in equal amounts to all my children, **OR**	
7. B*	Distribution of unequal amounts of income to my children is permitted.	
8. *	Up to 50% of the actual income received by the Trust can be distributed to my children upon the written instructions of my spouse without decreasing payments of my spouse's income. Distributions to my children over 50% of the actual income will reduce dollar for dollar the income my spouse is to receive that year.	
9. A *	When distributions of principal are made, they are to be made in equal amounts to all my children, **OR**	
9. B	Distribution of unequal amounts of principal to my children is permitted.	
10. *	My spouse shall have the right to direct that a beneficiary's share of income or principal from this Trust be held in Trust under terms and condition my spouse indicates. This includes a beneficiary's share upon my spouse's death.	
11.	My surviving spouse shall have the right to change the share each child and heir will receive upon my spouse's death.	

C. Family visits

Option	Description	Include
12.*	Trust is to pay reasonable travel expenses for visits by my children to my spouse when ill or in a nursing home.	
13.*	Trust shall also pay travel expenses for our Grandchildren's visits to my spouse.	
14. *	Trust to pay travel expenses for our children to attend spouse's funeral.	
15. *	My spouse shall have the authority to remove the trustee and appoint a new one.	

D. Trustee & Safeguarding Assets

Option	Description	Include
16.*	All assets in my Trust will be held by a bank acting as custodian or in a brokerage account.	
17. *	Copies of all reports of the custodian or brokerage firm are to be sent to my trustee and all my beneficiaries	
18. *	My trustee can change custodian or brokerage firm.	
19. *	All transfers of assets from custodians or brokerage houses are to be made directly to new custodian or broker.	

E. Trust Investments and Payments

Option	Description	Include
20. *	The initial investments of my Trust are as follows: Stocks_____%; Bonds_____%	
21. *	As stocks increase in value, do not sell them and buy bonds to re-balance my portfolio.	
22. *	Payments from principal are to be made from the proceeds of stock sales.	

F.   Imporatant Options to Include

Option	Description	Include
23. *	Ability to change the state that controls my Trust.	
24*	Include here the special needs of your family such as particular requirements for individual members, providing for special events, anticipating the unplanned or the unusual happenings that can occur in the lifetime of the family.	

Review some of the items in Chapter 11, such as <u>Anticipating probable needs</u> on page 108. Review any items you marked and notes you made as you read this book.

Remember, it is your money, you can control its future use. A key objective in all of your documents is to encourage the continuation of strong family relationships.

Survivor Notebook

<u>A need neglected by most advisors</u>

For whatever reasons, most preparers of estate plans and writers on topics of Saving Estate Taxes, Living Trusts and Avoiding Probate never cover one very important aspect: helping the surviving spouse and family members immediately following the death of a loved one. This can be accomplished by simply setting up in advance a list of what needs to be done and the location of key documents.

Many decisions that surviving family must make immediately after a person's death can be planned for now. The availability of funds for six months or more of expenses needs to be provided for, including funeral costs and family travel expenses. Lists of important contacts and phone numbers should be prepared. And, some advice, particularly to your wife as the surviving spouse should be given at this time.

<u>A planning check list</u>

These thing can be done now.

1.   Are all of your estate planning documents completed and up-to-date? If not, do it now.

2.   Prepare a notebok with your spouse, and other heirs, that contains all of the information they will need to know. A great deal of the required information such as the location of documents; insurance policies, key contacts (Social Security, Banks and Brokers, Veterans Administration, etc.) can be entered on forms available to you

from our web site (www.ccmtrust.com). These forms provide both a convenient place and a check list of items that must be considered.

3. Meet with a funeral director, tell the family what you had discussed and leave a note or copy of any agreement. This can be a great help to everyone. They will know what you want and can arrange it.

4. Financial Plans and Data.
    This form will provide a quick overview of your assets and help plan the start of estate tax reporting. A key part of this section is the availability of funds for the first six months after your death, including funeral expenses.

5. Investment Considerations.
    Your spouse needs to be familiar with your investments and should meet with your investment advisor and/or broker, as well as any representative of banks or other financial institutions you deal with while you are both well enough and capable enough to do it.

6. Other key considerations to do now:

    A). Obtain separate credit cards for your spouse. Your wife needs to establish a credit history.

    B). Select and meet with a friend or relative or a professional advisor who will assist your spouse. This person should be known to the spouse, not simply a name on a list.

C). Consider letters to your heirs regarding instructions and your wishes.

It is very important to consider leaving a memo for the family member or friend, who will serve as your trustee. Copies should go to the other adult family members or heirs.

Your trustee should be instructed to read the document and make notes on items questioned and then visit the attorney who prepared the Trust. If that attorney is no longer available, consult another.

To afford as clear an understanding as possible for all beneficiaries, have your trustee review with your heirs how the Trust will be managed, according to your directives and Trust law.

For additional information and suggestions, visit our web site www.ccmtrust.com./the book.

A Trust is a Contract

There are many different types of trusts. What they have in common is that each type of Trust is a contract. In the contract the terms and conditions are stated. The person administering a Trust contract is called a trustee. The beneficiaries of the Trust contract are called the remaindermen and the income beneficiary. A person called a grantor creates the Trust (contract) and places assets into the Trust.

The Basic Form of a Trust

Person:
a) Established a Trust
b) Funds the Trust

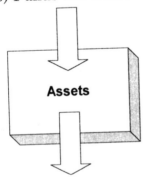

Beneficiaries

of the Trust

Note: Many Trusts are established in a person's Will or in their Living Trust

Assets are placed in the Trust. These can be cash, securities, real property or anything else of value. Assets may continue to be placed in the Trust.

Generally there are two types of beneficiaries of a Trust: 1) The person(s) who are to receive income from the Trust during their lifetime or for a stated period. And 2) the persons and organizations who receive the principal when the Trust is terminated.

The Purpose of a Trust

In the above diagram, a person established a Trust. Let's use the example of a man who wanted to provide after his death for the care of his wife. After his wife's death, he wanted to have the assets in the Trust given equally to his four children. The following are key questions that need to be asked and examples of answers.

What is the purpose of the Trust?

To provide a lifetime income for my wife's needs after my death.

After the purpose of the Trust is satisfied, who is to receive any assets left in the Trust?

They are to be divided equally among my four children. And, I may name other people and charities to receive a part of my Trust.

Who is to be the trustee of the Trust?

A Trust department of a bank or one of my children or a friend.

There are a few additional questions such as the age the children are to be when they receive their share of the Trust. But in most instances only the above three questions are presented. They, along with the answers given, are expected to supply a body of information from which can be prepared a financially effective Trust.

But unfortunately, the answer to the first question *"What is the purpose of the Trust"* is often forgotten at the time the Trust is prepared. Problems can and do result in the document itself and for the family it is supposed to protect and benefit. More information must be requested and supplied.

Some key questions never asked are:

1. *What will be the specific income needs of your wife after your death?*

2. *What portion of her income needs must come from the Trust?*

Most people never ask or plan for the answers to these last two questions. The wife's income needs from the Trust were never discussed with the preparer of the Trust.

The explanation given by most people is that they thought the income their surviving spouse would receive was controlled by Trust law and the tax code. They did not know that they had an option in determining exactly what that amount would be.

Most people who invest their money want to know about return, safety and growth in value.

However, when it came to investing $675,000 or more of family assets in a Trust, they never directed a single question to these important factors. In short they chose to disregard their usual fiscal discipline of return, safety and growth. This was a failure at a crucial time: a time when they were making an important investment decision. As a result, the Trust prepared for them was "silent."[1] It was silent on how

(1)   "Silent" is a legal term meaning that the document neglected to state what the Grantor wanted. As a result the "Default Rules" of the state will determine and govern these issues the grantor neglected.

the funds in the Trust would be invested; silent on the annual income their surviving spouse (the income beneficiary) would receive; and silent on an estimated end-value of the Trust for their children (the remaindermen).

Most people are shocked to learn that if they placed $625,000 in a Trust for the support of their wife, she would only receive about $19,000 a year from that Trust, further reduced by state and federal income taxes. But this is what can happen.

The reason is the Trust investments are determined by the Default Rules. Today's low interest and dividend rates give the surviving spouse an annual income of about 3.0% of the value of the Trust. Such a meager income can result if the options available are not used when preparing a Trust.

As mentioned in the first part of this chapter, under the current federal estate-tax rates, each person can leave up to $625,000 free of federal estate taxes in 1998. This amount increases to $ 1 million in 2006.

Many people establish a Credit Shelter Trust because they want to take maximum advantage of their lifetime federal estate-tax credit.

When a husband and wife each establish a Credit Shelter Trust, they can shelter $1.35 million of their assets by combining their individual $675,000 exemptions in 2001. For a couple who does this, their combined federal estate-tax exemption increases to $ 2 million in 2006. And can continue to increase with new federal estate-tax laws.

Establishing Credit Shelter Trusts

The husband has a Will prepared and the wife
has a Will prepared. In each Will a Trust is established
with the maximum amount of an individual's federal
estate-tax exemption. Each Will states that at their
death their maximum exemption from federal estate
taxes is to be placed in a Trust for their children (or
others) and the income paid to their surviving spouse.
This is shown below.

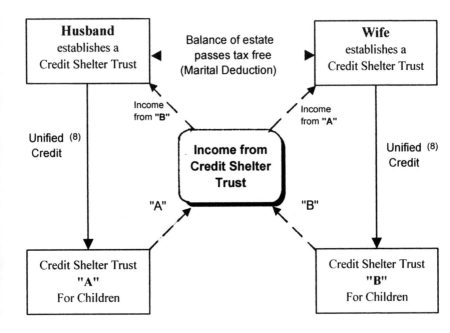

(8)   The Unified Credit is the term the federal government uses
in the estate-tax code. It is this tax credit that allows each
individual to leave $ 675,000 free of federal estate taxes in
2001. This amount increases in the following years to
$ 1 million in 2006.

Notes: 1. In the event the husband dies first, his Credit Shelter Trust "A" is established and the income from his Trust is paid to his wife. In this case, the wife's Credit Shelter Trust "B" is no longer required since her husband has died.

2. If the wife had died first, her Bypass Trust "B" is established and the income from her Trust is paid to her husband. In this case, the husband's Credit Shelter Trust "A" is no longer required since his wife has died.

When the above Credit Shelter Trusts are written, both the husband and the wife are alive and able to execute legal documents. Each document generally states that if that person dies first, the maximum amount of their assets allowed under the Unified Credit are to be placed in their Credit Shelter Trust. It is to be held there for the benefit of their children and the income is to be paid to the surviving spouse.

After the death of the surviving spouse, the funds in the Trust are given to their children or any other persons or organizations, such as a charity, according to the terms of their Credit Shelter Trust.

In most cases, the first to die is the husband. At that time, his Credit Shelter Trust is activated. All or part of the other assets the husband has can pass tax free directly to his wife. Or, he could have placed all or some of the assets in a Marital Trust. These assets would also pass tax free at the time of his death. But the assets that remain in the Marital Trust may be taxed at the time of the wife's death if, combined with her other assets, they exceed her Unified Credit.

When she dies, up to $675,000 of her estate in 2001 (allowed by the Unified Credit) goes tax free to the children. In 2006 and after, this amount is $ 1 million.

Combining the husband's federal estate-tax credit with the wife's tax credit results in providing $1.35 million in 2001 that they can leave free of federal estate taxes. In later years this amount is scheduled to increase.

By doing this, the couple save at least $235,000 in federal estate taxes. There can also be an additional tax saving based on the estate-tax rates of most states.

Trusts to be funded after the death of a person are generally documented in that person's Last Will and Testament. There is the option of establishing a Living Trust while you are alive that can also establish a Credit Shelter Trust and other Trusts after your death. Living Trusts are generally established to avoid probate and can have other advantages over a Trust established in your Will.

You can also establish an Irrevocable Trust and many other kinds of Trusts during your lifetime. Trust attorneys are well versed in all of the different types of Trusts available to you. The important issue in planning a Trust is determining what you want to accomplish with your estate. This requires decisions that can only be made by you. The financial and management options available to you and placed in your Trust will then make it an effective document.

Duties of a Trustee

Introduction

The prime duty of a trustee is the investment management of the funds in the Trust and other types of assets that may be a part of the Trust such as real property. Some professional trustees will only manage the investment of funds. Others will also manage real estate such as homes, rental properties, vacant land, timber interests, oil and minerals.

Next, the trustee must know the laws regarding Trusts and properly administer the Trust according to these laws. And, annually your trustee must file state and federal fiduciary tax returns. These are the prime duties of a trustee.

Overshadowing the above and all other duties of the trustee is the duty of loyalty. It means loyalty to serve the wishes of the decedent and loyalty to serve the beneficiaries of the Trust. This is an important duty. Acts that may appear to be innocent of any personal gain by the use of the position of trustee may be declared by the courts to be a violation of this duty of loyalty.

The Duty of Loyalty

A trustee must not use the assets in a Trusts for their benefit - either directly or indirectly. Numerous court cases have ruled against trustees for violating this duty of loyalty. For example:

A trustee himself may wish to purchase from the Trust an asset such as real estate, art or other personal property. The trustee may have paid the highest price for an asset (an important duty of a trustee is to obtain the highest price for the sale of any asset), but courts have ruled against trustees who have purchased Trust assets sold at auction, even when the trustee was the highest bidder.[A-1]

And, if the property at some later time increases in value, the beneficiaries can recover the property. Or, if the property were sold, the beneficiaries can obtain the profit from the sale.

There are ways that the purchase of assets from the Trust by the trustee can be properly done. The laws and procedures for this vary by states. An Attorney should be consulted.[2]

"The fiduciary (trustee) always has the burden of proving full disclosure in dealing with beneficiaries and, in the situation where the fiduciary (trustee) is also a beneficiary, the further burden of showing that the transaction is fair to the other beneficiaries" [A-2] [B-1]

So wide and far reaching is the duty of loyalty that a co-trustee who knows that another co-trustee has failed in a duty of loyalty is also guilty of that failure and is legally accountable.

A-1)   Numerous legal books on Trusts cite many court rulings and regulations regarding a trustee's duty of loyalty. A few of these books are mentioned at the end of this Appendix. And, reference to acts of trustees are by letter footnote for each book.

(2)   This is just another of the many reasons why a family member or friend serving as trustee, must continually consult an attorney.

Co-trustees may divide minor trustee matters. "As to more important matters, however, one co-trustee cannot act alone. Unanimous agreement and action is required and for most decisions should be in writing and signed by both parties"[A-3] [B-2] This can happen when family members are co-trustees. Example:

Family co-trustees decide that one trustee will handle the investments and the other co-trustee will perform other duties - perhaps looking after the income beneficiary. But if the second co-trustee "was not exercising any control over the selection of investments . . (they) clearly breached (their) duties to act prudently and to perform (their) duties as a trustee. . . . A Fiduciary my not delegate to another the performance of a duty involving discretion and judgment." [A-4]

In most cases where a family member is the trustee, they are also a beneficiary of the trust.

The trustee may not favor one beneficiary at the expense of another. A son, as trustee, may not favor his mother, as the surviving spouse and income beneficiary, over his brothers and sisters and other heirs who will receive the funds in the Trust at the death of the surviving spouse.[B-3]

A trustee, especially a family member, has the added liability of documenting that each action taken was fair to all beneficiaries.

"It is important that he or she carefully preserve throughout the administration a record of activities. If the fiduciary is unable to explain or justify his or her acts, the fiduciary may be liable."[A-5]

The above should clearly indicate that it is very important for the Grantor to clearly state in their Trust what they want to have happen. A Grantor should state the income their surviving spouse is to receive, how the funds are to be invested, and many other provisions recommended in this book.

Then the trustee will be following the grantor's instructions stated in the Trust. A trustee must do this, follow the grantor's instructions.

"Except where impossible, illegal, or where a change of circumstances occurs which would impair the purposes of the Trust, the nature and extent of the duties and powers of a trustee are determined by the Trust instrument." [A-6]

A Trustee's Greatest Problem - Managing the Investments.

Most legal action against a trustee, excluding fraud and other violations of loyalty, will be in the area of investments. And, a trustee may have the greatest problem in defending these types of suits.

In addition to carefully maintaining documented notes on all of their acts, especially those regarding investments, a family member or friend serving as trustee is encouraged to seek investment advice.

The new Uniform Prudent Investor Act (UPIA) strongly encourages a family member or friend to hire a professional trustee to manage the investments of the assets in the Trust.

So important did the drafters and the legislative bodies of the states consider the need for professional management of the investments in a Trust that they broke new legal ground and granted an exception in the new UPIA to the long standing rule of trustee responsibility. The new law relieves the trustee of any liability resulting from investing if the delegation was properly made. [3]

This is new law. The law in the past has always stated that responsibility cannot be delegated and the trustee who gives discretionary power to another is liable for the acts of another who has been given this delegated power.

But now, an important responsibility of a trustee in modern day Trusts, the investment of Trust assets, may be delegated and if properly done, the trustee is relieved of any legal liability.

Grantors should consider the reasons for this new law, and the relief it offers a family member or friend as trustee. It would be better if the grantor selected the professional trustee rather than have a family member, years later make the selection of the investment manager.

This would allow the grantor to select a professional manager whose fees are reasonable and whose past investment performance would indicate proper handling of the assets.

(3)   See Section 9 of the Uniform Prudent Investor Act in Appendix F and the commentary on this section

Summary

The law regarding a trustee's duties is extensive. Most professional trustees understand these legal responsibilities. Few family members or friends, serving as trustees, do.

That is why every individual serving as a trustee should quickly obtain the assistance of a competent Trust attorney before making any decisions as trustee. The special powers given to a trustee is in the document that created the Trust and the person named as trustee must follow these specific directives in the Trust document. But there are numerous other legal and tax requirements that govern the work of a trustee not stated in the Trust document.

An experienced Trust attorney can interpret and guide an individual trustee in understanding the specific directives in a Trust that must be followed. The assistance of this Trust attorney is particularly important in helping the individual understand the other problems that can result from the legal and tax requirements that govern the work of a trustee but that are not stated in the Trust document.

Proper documentation of the actions of a trustee is required.

Review the reasons for this new "Uniform Prudent Investors Act" and the relief it offers a family member or friend as trustee.

The grantor should consider leaving a memo for their family member or friend selected to be their trustee. The memo would contain instructions and suggestions regarding their Trust. The first and most important instruction to the trustee would be to:

First: Before taking any action as trustee:

A.   Read the Trust document and make notes on any items you have questions about.

B.   Then visit my attorney who prepared my Trust and review these items.

C.   Ask the attorney what changes have been made in any regulations that you should be aware of. Ask for recommendations concerning other items of your trusteeship that you should know about.

D.   Obtain assistance in obtaining the tax I.D. number for the Trust and how to properly accept the assets to be paced in the Trust.

E.   Obtain   advice   on   your   record - keeping responsibilities as Trustee. Everything you do should be properly documented and saved during the life of the Trust.

Second: Determine what other professional assistance you will need as Trustee.

A.   Proper state and federal tax forms must be filed. Obtain the assistance of a CPA who has experience in filing these forms.

B.   Their may be other professionals recommended for your consideration whose services may be needed.   Property Appraisers, Investment Advisors, etc.

Third: After you as my trustee have obtained the above guidance and understand what is to be done:

A.   Review the Trust with my income beneficiary (surviving spouse) and the remaindermen (my Children and other heirs); how it will be managed, according to my directives and Trust law.

B.   While not stated in the Trust, my hope is that a strong family relationship will be maintained.

References:

(A)   "Decedents' Estates and Trusts" by John Ritchie, Neill H. Alford, Jr., Richard W. Effland and Joel C. Dobris, The Foundation Press, Inc. Westbury, New York Eighth Edition, 1993.

Used as a casebook for law students in wills, trusts, fiduciary administration and future interests. 1445 pages.

Footnotes to the above casebook are:

> (A-1) Page 1247
> (A-2) Page 1248
> (A-3) Page 1252
> (A-4) Page 1254
> (A-5) Page 1260
> (A-6) Page 1265

B) "Loring A Trustee's Handbook" 1997 Edition
     Charles E. Rounds, Jr., Little Brown and
     Company, New York

> Designed as a handbook for ready
> reference to be "user friendly." 352 pages

Footnotes to the above handbook are:

> (B-1) Page 20
> (B-2) Page 34
> (B-3) Page 21

APPENDIX C

Understanding Default Rules
That Control Trusts

Introduction

State Default Rules are not the cause of financial and management problems in Trusts. In fact, they are often the only thing that keeps a Trust instrument from failing. When a Trust fails because of a lack of specific instructions, those assets in it revert to the estate and pass by Will or intestacy.

When a Trust is silent on important issues that the grantor neglected in their Trust, direction is provided by Default Rules. These Rules have been passed by each state's legislative branch in the United States and there are changes continually being proposed.[1]

An example of this work is the requirement in the new Uniform Prudent Investor Act for trustees to diversify the investments in a Trust. This is based on modern portfolio theory. A second act, The Uniform Principal and Income Act (1997)[2] was recently approved and is currently recommended for enactment

(1)　In the United States the National Conference of Commissioners on Uniform State Laws, a confederation of state commissioners on uniform laws was founded in 1892. Its membership comprises more than 300 attorneys, judges and law professors who are appointed by each of the 50 states, the District of Columbia, Puerto Rico and the U. S Virgin Islands, to draft uniform and model state laws and work toward their enactment.

(2)　This new Act and comments on it are available on the Internet at site of the National Conference of Commissioners on Uniform State Laws at "www.law.upenn.edu/bll."

in all the states. Both of these uniform acts are Default Rules designed to improve Trust investments and income paid when the Grantor fails to state what is required in the Trust. Neither of these acts provide the financial and management options a grantor has that are presented in this book.

If the grantor neglects to direct the trustee on how the funds are to be invested, then the Default Rules will govern this issue. In general the reasoning behind these Default Rules, while perhaps conservative in nature, has been well thought out.

To assist in Trust situations where there is a lack of investment instructions, the Default Rules for investments were developed in response to the logical conclusion that since the Trust was silent, the investments should favor neither the income beneficiary nor the remaindermen. Bonds produce a higher income, this favors the income beneficiary. Stocks while increasing in value over time (that would favor the remaindermen), will produce a lower income. As a result, an equitable Default Rule for investments was written.

The Default Rules state - invest approximately 50% of the Trust in bonds and 50% of the Trust in stocks for a "Balanced Trust." As a result of this reasoning, it would appear that the investments of the Trust would favor neither the income beneficiary nor the remaindermen.

The real point is that in our modern world, inflation is as great a danger as losing an investment outright. There is as great a risk of falling behind as there is of losing an investment. The Default Rules generally address the second of these two concerns because they are heavily influenced by conservative attitudes regarding investments. This does not make them wrong. It makes them conservative, as far as investments are concerned. The reader should be aware of their own right to balance their own levels of risk and growth.

In this sense the Default Rules do not lower growth or income. The grantor has simply lost the opportunity to decide in their Trust whether they prefer and are comfortable with their own investment options that allow more potential for growth.

The critical point however, is that the grantor, as their own financial planner, has to be the one who chooses the level of risk they are willing to balance against growth. They already do this with the investments they make in their normal lives.

Another critical option the grantor has is determining the annual payments to the income beneficiary (generally the surviving spouse) from the Trust.

As indicated in Chapter 7, if the Grantor does not plan and use their option of stating the annual payments to be made from their Trust, the actual amounts that will be paid are generally the Net Income[3] from the investments of the Trust. That means that half of the fees and expenses to manage the trust are deducted form the Gross Income. This is not recommended.

This is generally a lower amount than may be required for the surviving spouse. The grantor had the option of planning the income needs and increasing it for inflation and using their option of stating this in their Trust.

Also the grantor has the option of giving directives in the Trust that can increase the value of it for their children and other heirs. See Chapter 10.

Other options a grantor has are summarized in the check list in Chapter 19.

Default Rules Referenced in Trusts

You will find included in your executed Trust an article, generally toward the end of the document. It makes reference to the state your Trust was constructed in along with a listing of the statutes of the state that become part of your Trust. You can read these state statutes (also called Default Rules) that are part of your Trust in your attorney's office or they can be found in the reference section of most libraries.

You may not agree with some of the Default Rules you will read. But remember, they were written to be broad enough in scope to cover many situations Trustees may face.

As examples of trustee powers that are in Default Rules and that you may not want in your Trust are:[4]

1.   To invest in such assets as the trustee shall

(4)   General Statutes of North Carolina, Chapter 32-27, Items (3) and (4).

deem advisable, even though such investments shall not be of the character approved by applicable law but for this provision.

2. To invest without diversification by making investments which cause a greater proportion of the property held by the trustee to be invested in instruments of one type or of one company.

For most people these powers would not be applicable. A professional trustee would not use them. Some could be considered significant in the case of a closely held family business that the grantor intended to have remain in the family.

The shares would eventually pass to the remaindermen after the death of the surviving spouse.

One could say that in such an instance, the grantor should have used their option of stating in the Trust, wording that would accomplish this objective. But in the past, even when the grantor had a family business, this directive may have been left out. This is just one example of why such broad authority can be found in state statutes.

Annually Evaluating the Investment
Performance of the Trustee.

Introduction

Every investor should measure the performance of their investments. Professional investors and advisors continually do this but most individual investors do not devote full time to managing their investments. But they should measure the performance of their investments at least each quarter or semi-annually. This is especially important to do for common stock investments. The same concept of measuring performance applies to investments in a Trust that may be held by others as trustee.

If a bank Trust department is your trustee, information on the results of other banks can be obtained to compare their trustee performance compared to yours. This is especially important for that portion of the Trust invested in common stocks.

How to measure the performance of your stocks.

The key measurement of the performance of stocks is the S&P 500 index (Standard & Poor). It is composed of the S & P 400 Industrials, the S & P 20 Transportation, the S & P 40 Financial and the S & P 40 Utilities.

Most of the stocks in the S & P 500 are found on the New York Stock Exchange, though there are a few from the American Stock Exchange and the over-the-counter markets.

The S&P 500 index represents about 80 percent of the market value of all the issues traded on the NYSE. The S & P is commonly considered the benchmark against which the performance of individual stocks or stock groups is measured. It is a far broader measure of market activity than the DJIA (Dow Jones Industrial Average), even through the DJIA is quoted more widely.

Not matter who is controlling or advising you on the stocks that are purchased and sold, such as in a retirement account, a mutual fund, a Trust account or your personal account, the actual performance of your stocks should be measured against the performance of the S & P 500.

The two main investment vehicles for a trustee are stocks and bonds. Investments in stocks are made based on the belief that the total return (dividends plus the growth in value), over time, will far exceed the return from bonds. Trustees do not invest in bonds for the growth of the investment. Speculation in bond futures, because of the high risks, is not an activity a trustee should engage in. Investments in bonds are made to obtain a higher interest income [1] than dividends provide.

Separate measurements are to be made of the investment results of the funds invested in stocks and the funds invested in bonds.

(1)   Investment in bonds carry an inflationary and interest rate risk. With inflation, the purchasing power of the funds invested in bonds are reduced. Even at a low inflationary rate of 3% a year, the purchasing power of bonds decreases in value 48% every twenty years.

To Measure the Investment Performance of U.S. Traded Stocks.

The S & P 500 index is used to measure the investment performance of stocks. It is considered the "market" and is the benchmark to which the performance of s stock portfolio is to be measured and compared. To make this measurement only a few facts are required and they are illustrated below.

1. Value of the stock holdings,
   December 22, 1999 $ 763,500
   Less: Stock Value when Trust
   funded, January 3, 1997   - 430,000
       Unadjusted Gain in Account $ 333,500
       Percent Gain   77.6%

2. S&P 500 Index, Close December 22, 1999   1,456
   Less: Index when Trust funded,
       Close January 3, 1997   - 748
       Increase in the index   708
       Percent Gain   94.7%

In the above example, the SP 500 index appears to have outperformed the trustee's investments in stocks. But the above example was not adjusted to make a true comparison. An adjustment is required for withdrawals. These withdrawals are for any trustee fees and expenses and payments of principal made to the surviving spouse that were charged to the stock portion of the Trust portfolio.

The above example has not been adjusted to take into account any withdrawals against the stock investments. This adjustment is made below.

1.   Unadjusted Stock Gain in Trust $ 333,500
        Adjustments:
        withdrawals charged against stocks:
        a. 1995 withdrawals $14,754
        b. 1996 withdrawals   31,379
        c. 1997 withdrawals   43,560
                Total Withdrawals   + $ 89,693
        Gross Gain in Stocks $ 423,193

This adjusted gain is now the basis for comparison:

1. Value of the stock holdings,
    December 22, 1999 $ 763,500
    Plus: Withdrawals charged against stocks + $ 89,693
                Total $ 853,193
    Less: Stock Value when Trust
            funded, January 3, 1997   - 430,000
        Adjusted Gain in Stocks $ 423,193
                Percent Gain   98.4%

On an adjusted basis, the trustee's investment performance was slightly better than the benchmark, the S&P 500 that gained 88.5%. No consideration should be given to replacing the trustee provided the gains were not made from very speculative stocks which would not normally be the case with a bank or other professional trustee.

Trustees who invest under the new Uniform Prudent Investors Act (UPIA in Appendix E) are required to achieve broad diversification in their stock holdings. To accomplish this, mutual funds or index funds are generally used. But there will still be cases in which individual stocks will be held.

A second level of measurement of the investment performance of stocks is to look at the investment return of each component in the stock portfolio measured to the S&P 500 index. These components might be several mutual funds and individual stocks. An example of this measurement follows:

Shares	STOCKS	Market Start Date	Value Ending Date	% Gain
1500	Fund "A"	$136,121	$ 174,643	28.30%
1200	Fund "B"	124,743	155,854	25.55%
1440	Fund "C"	147,498	168,605	14.31%
480	Bristol Myers	21,600	39,420	82.50%
800	Coca Cola	39,200	56,800	44.90%
225	Eastman Kodak	17,494	17,663	0.96%
400	Exxon	17,375	24,175	39.14%
800	General Electric	34,700	52,250	50.58%
600	Hershey Foods	22,012	33,975	54.35%
400	Intel	29,375	56,900	93.70%
500	McDonalds	23,375	24,312	4.01%
500	Merck	32,312	51,250	58.61%
200	Mobil Corp	11,237	13,875	23.48%
500	Pfizer	35,687	61,000	70.93%
100	Procter & Gamble	9,062	13,931	53.73%
100	Schlumberger	8,425	12,500	48.3%
	TOTALS	$ 710,216	$ 957,153	34.77%
S & P 500 Index		671	848	26.45%

The above analysis indicates that the growth of the Trust's total equity portfolio exceeded the S&P 500

(2) The above Table lists market prices for the mutual funds, individual stocks, the S & P 500 and their percent gains. This was done to illustrate a method for reviewing individual funds and securities held in a portfolio.

index over the last 12 months. However, the purpose of the above example is to compare how individual mutual funds and stocks performed over this time period.

The stock market is very efficient. The market prices the stocks daily based on all available information. Therefore, it is best to assume that the market has priced each stock based on its value. There are exceptions, particularly for small companies, and occasionally with a medium and even a large company.

Therefore, the above illustration indicates that Mutual Fund "C," Eastman Kodak and McDonalds require special attention. What is the "market" telling us about Mutual Fund "C" and these two stocks? Why has Mutual Fund "C" only increased 14.31% compared to a 26.45% increase in the S&P 500 index.?

Was this a Mutual Fund that invested in a special sector such as small stocks, international stocks, etc.? Or, is it a case of poor fund management ? How well has this fund performed over the last three or five years?   Should this fund be sold?

SUMMARY - On Measuring the Investment Performance of Stocks in a Trust.

1.   Every Grantor of a Trust should give serious consideration to naming a trustee who has the knowledge, experience and time to properly invest and manage the assets in his Trust.

2.   Each Trust should give the surviving spouse, or some other person, the power to replace the trustee.

3.   In addition, a Grantor should consider leaving written instructions on how evaluations are to be made of the trustee's investment performance. Others in the family or friends can then assist the person, who has the authority to replace a trustee, with this evaluation.

4.   Special and extra attention is generally given by the trustee who knows that their investment performance is being monitored.

There are measurements for other types of equity investments such as small cap stocks (Wilshire 4500), international stocks by country and areas of the world. But for most stock investors, the S&P 500 is the index to use. A listing of "Examples of Other Types of Equity Measurements" and "To Measure the Investment Performance of Bonds" is in our web site: www.ccmtrust .com.

APPENDIX E

Fees & Services of Professional Trustees

Introduction

Over 80% of Trusts do not use a professional trustee. A family member or friend is the trustee. Why? In most cases the grantor:

1. Believes the fees professional trustees charge are high.

2. Does not understand the financial benefits to their surviving spouse and child of using a professional trustee to manage the investments.

3. Believes that the care and concerns a family member can provide to their surviving spouse and other heirs are more important than the investment expertise of a professional trustee.

4. Places the assets in the Trust without further safeguards for the protection of the assets and the family.

All of the above four points will be discussed. Hopefully after reviewing this material, a grantor will give serious consideration to a professional trustee. Their annual fees can be as low as half a percent a year.

1. The Grantor Believes the Fees Professional Trustees Charge Are High.

Professional trustees are able to manage the investments in securities for a low fee. The reason for these low fees is that actual costs today, to manage these investments is spread over a large number of Trusts.

The new requirements for investing Trust assets under the Uniform Prudent Investor Act (see Appendix E) is that the principles of modern portfolio theory are to be observed. No longer is an individual portfolio of eight or ten stocks considered to be properly diversified to protect the principal of the Trust.

Professional trustee management of investments has been moving away from individual securities placed in a Trust. Today, under modern portfolio theory, diversified groupings of similar types of securities are being selected.

If good quality bonds are required in the Trust, the selection is shifting from purchasing individual bonds to be placed in the Trust to allocating shares of a good quality bond fund centrally managed. The same is true of stocks.

These funds hold a large number of bonds or stocks to provide a greater diversification. Index funds are also used.

The result of this movement toward placing shares of mutual funds and index funds into Trusts has been a reduction in the cost of managing the investment function. The fees can be lower.

Rather than reviewing and perhaps changing the individual securities held in each Trust, this function is now centralized.

One example of reduced fees is shown in the fee schedule below.

Trust Assets	Annual Fee[1]	Value of Trust		
		$675,000	$ 2 million	$ 4 million
First $1 million	0.65%	$4,388	$ 6,500	$ 6,500
Next $1million	0.35%		3,500	3,500
Over $2 million	0.20%			4,000
Total Annual Fee		$ 4,388	$ 10,000	$ 14,000
Percent of Total Assets		0.65%	0.50%	0.35%
Minimum Annual Fee			$ 3,250	

But if the Trust directs the holding of individual securities, which will increase the cost of investment management, an additional annual fee of 0.30% will be charged.

Another key point that needs to be considered is the management and other charges associated with the Trust owning fund shares. In many cases, not only are the annual fees of mutual funds not considered but the costs of buying and selling securities are not evaluated by the grantor in determining who will manage the investments.

A family member or friend named as trustee will incur these transaction costs in managing the

[1]   Source: Trust Fees of Vanguard Personal Trust Services as of March, 2001

investments. But these costs are overlooked by the grantor or rarely considered.

Many professional trustees may not accept real estate as a Trust asset that they will manage. Therefore their fees may be lower since managing real estate requires different skills and generally a higher fee for the added expense.

Trustees may also charge an additional amount for fiduciary tax return preparation, court accounting (if required). All of these items need to be considered. Generally if this work is required of the professional trustee, a family member, serving as trustee, will also be required to have the same work done. And, the expense can be greater.

The fee schedule of a typical bank for personal Trust services is an annual fee as a percent of the market value of the account..

Market Value of Assets	Annual Fee	Value of Trust		
		$675,000	$1 million	$2 million
$400,000 to $700,000	1.0%%	$ 6,750	$ 6,750	$ 6,750
$700,000 to $1.0 million	0.9%	—	2,700	2,700
$1 million to $2 million	0.7%	—	____	7,000
Total Annual Fee		$ 6,250	$ 9,4 50	$ 16,450
Percent of Total Assets		1.0%	0.95%	0.82%

Minimum Annual Fee varies, generally at least $2,000. Banks may charge additional fees for some special services:

1.   For management of illiquid assets, such as real estate, closely-held business interests, notes and liabilities. The annual fee may be 2% of the market value.

2.   If a co-trustee is used, along with the bank, some banks may charge an additional fee for the extra work required to obtain the co-trustees approval of any investment decisions. Generally this fee is very small and is waived for Trusts of $1 million or more.

3.   For the purchase or sale of illiquid assets an additional fee may also be charged.

All of the above items are in bank's fee schedules that a Grantor should review.

2. The Grantor Does Not Understand the Financial Benefits of Using a Professional Trustee to Manage the Investments.

Most professional trustees publish the performance of their Trust investments. And for most, the performance is compared to recognized benchmarks such the S & P 500 index (Standard and Poor) for Equity Funds and several Lehman Government/Corporate bond indexes for various bond funds.[2]

(2)   These measurements of investment performance are similar to what is recommended in Appendix D.

You can obtain copies free of charge. The investment results by these professional trustees may outperform what an individual trustee may obtain. And, the investments will be diversified.

The evaluation a Grantor needs to make is who can provide the highest reasonable investment returns for my Trust. The amounts involved are large. A 10% upward movement for a $1 million dollar Trust is $100,000. Who can best accomplish this - a professional trustee or my family member trustee?

A Trust should contain a provision for the removal of the professional trustee and appointing a new one (see Chapter 9). Perhaps the family member being considered as trustee could better serve as the watchdog of a professional trustee's performance.

3.   That the Care and Concerns a Family Member can Provide to Their Surviving Spouse and other Heirs are More Important Than the Investment Expertise of a Professional Trustee.

This is true. A family member can, in most cases, do a much better job and will usually have greater concern for the surviving spouse and other heirs than a professional trustee.

As stated in Chapter 9, the care, advice and comfort given to your surviving spouse are best done by family members and friends. There is no requirement that only your trustee should do this for your surviving spouse. A professional trustee can provide some of this type of assistance, when nursing homes and other care is required for the survivor. But again, family members can best handle this need and look to the trustee to pay the bills, if needed.

The Grantor Can Consider a "Special Trustee."

You can provide in your Trust for a "Special Trustee(s)" such as family members or friends whose responsibilities are clearly stated in the Trust and are different from the traditional role of a trustee. These "Special Trustee(s)" would have responsibilities such as, the care, advice and comfort given to your surviving spouse or other Income Beneficiaries.

If a nursing home or other medical care is required for the surviving spouse or Income Beneficiaries, this person would visit the nursing home to ensure that proper care was being given. This person would also have the Health Care Power of Attorney. Funds can be provided from the Trust for compensation for the "Special Trustee" and reasonable expenses could be automatically provided from the Trust for presents, travel expenses, etc. if needed.

4. The Grantor can place the assets in the Trust without further safeguards for them that we recommend when a family member is the trustee.

In Chapter 15, it was recommended that all funds and securities in the Trust are to be held by an appropriate custodian or at least be held in a brokerage account.

When a professional trustee is used, this custodial function is performed. For additional information on this recommendation, review Chapter 15.

Uniform Prudent Investors Act (UPIA)

Introduction

This Act is part of a group of "Uniform Acts" adopted by many states. The states that have adopted this new uniform act are listed on Page 211. The Act is short and clearly written. It breaks new ground in Trust law. It relieves your trustee of the legal liability for investment decisions if they properly delegate the investment responsibilities to a professional trustee. This is stated in Section 9 of the Act.

An important reason the Act was created was to recognize modern investment techniques that can protect the investment assets in the Trust. Several individuals were awarded Nobel prizes for their work on these investment techniques now required in the Act.

A portfolio consisting of eight or ten stocks is not properly diversified for protection of the assets. Modern portfolio theory requires a wide range of securities such as those found in mutual funds and index funds. It also requires awareness of international securities.

The Act establishes investment requirements for your trustee that they must follow if they choose to manage the investable assets in the Trust. It would appear that failure to follow these investment requirements in the Act could be grounds for legal action against a trustee.

The Act clearly states that your son, daughter or friend that you select as your trustee "is not liable to the beneficiaries or to the trust for decisions or actions of the agent to whom the function was delegated."[1]

The Act, in the beginning Sections makes clear the investment responsibilities of your trustee. These are:

1.   ". . to comply with the prudent investor rule set forth in this [Act]" See: Section 1 (a).

2.   To follow the standards of care; portfolio strategy; risk and return objectives set forth in Section 2 of the Act.

This would appear to require your trustee to have a written plan for the investment and management of the assets and to include in that plan "an overall investment strategy having risk and return objectives reasonably suited to the trust." [2]

Also to be included in the trustee's plan are requirements for the recognition of several planning factors such as general economic conditions; expected tax consequences; expected total return from income and the appreciation of capital and five other requirements set forth in the Act. [3]

3. Diversification of the assets as stated in Section 3.

(1)   See Section 9 (c) of the Act on the following pages.

(2)   From Section 2 (b) of the Act.

(3)   See Section (c) of the Act.

4.   To do this work of establishing an investment
plan to include the items required in the Act
within a reasonable time after becoming your
trustee. [4]

The Act also makes reference to the issue of
Loyalty of your trustee. This is a very important legal
requirement and is discussed in Appendix F.

"This [Act] applies to trusts existing on and
created after its effective date *(the date adopted by your
state)*. As applied to trusts existing on its effective date,
this [Act] governs only decisions or actions occurring
after that date." [5]

In Summary, What does this Act Require the Grantor to Consider?

1.   The Grantor can override this Act by Directives
placed in the Trust. This is allowed since the Act
is a Default Rule as clearly stated in Section 1
(b).

2.   However, the investment principals of
diversification and other requirements in the Act
such as having an investment plan containing
the items required by the Act, are sound and
should be considered.

3.   The Grantor after reviewing the Act may decide
that they will name in their Trust the

(4)   See Section 4 of the Act.

(5)   See Section 11 of the Act

professional investment manager they want to have handle their Trust instead of passing this decision to their trustee.

4.   If the Grantor's state has not yet adopted this Uniform Act, the Grantor can select what sections of the Act they want to include in their Trust.

Uniform Prudent Investors Act (UPIA)

SECTION 1. PRUDENT INVESTOR RULE.

(a)   Except as otherwise provided in subsection (b), a trustee who invests and manages assets owes a duty to the beneficiaries of the trust to comply with the prudent investor rule set forth in this [Act].

(b)   The prudent investor rule, a default rule, may be expanded, restricted, eliminated. or otherwise altered by the provisions of a trust. A trustee is not liable to a beneficiary to the extent that the trustee acted in reasonable reliance on the provisions of the trust.

SECTION 2. STANDARD OF CARE; PORTFOLIO STRATEGY; RISK AND RETURN OBJECTIVES

(a) A trustee shall invest and manage trust assets as a prudent investor would, by considering the purposes, terms, distribution requirements, and other circumstances of the trust. In satisfying this standard, the trustee shall exercise reasonable care, skill, and caution.

(b) A trustee's investment and management decisions must be evaluated not in isolation but in the context of the trust portfolio as a whole and as a part of an overall investment strategy having risk and return objectives reasonably suited to the trust.

(c) Among circumstances that a trustee shall consider in investing and managing assets are such of the following as are relevant to the trust or its beneficiaries:
(1) general economic conditions;

(2) the possible effect of inflation or deflation;

(3) the expected tax consequences of investment decisions or strategies;

(4) the role that each investment or course of action plays within the overall trust portfolio, which may include financial assets, interests in

closely held enterprises, tangible and intangible personal property, and real property;

(5) The expected total return from income and the appreciation of capital;

(6) other resources of the beneficiaries;

(7) needs for liquidity, regularity of income, and preservation or appreciation of capital; and

(8) an asset's special relationship or special value, if any, to the purpose of the trust or to one or more of the beneficiaries.

(d) A trustee shall make a reasonable effort to verify facts relevant to the investment and management of trust assets.

(e) A trustee may invest in any kind of property or type of investment consistent with the standards of this [Act].

(f) A trustee who has special skill or expertise, or is named trustee in reliance upon the trustee's representation that the trustee has special skill or expertise, has a duty to use those special skills or expertise.

SECTION 3. DIVERSIFICATION.

A trustee shall diversify the investments of the trust unless the trustee reasonably determines that, because of special circumstances, the purposes of the trust are better served without diversifying.

SECTION 4. DUTIES AT INCEPTION OF TRUSTEESHIP

Within a reasonable time after accepting a trusteeship or receiving trust assets, a trustee shall review the trust assets and make and implement decisions concerning the retention and disposition of assets, in order to bring the trust portfolio into compliance with the purposes, terms, distribution requirements, and other circumstances of the trusts, and within the requirements of this Act.

SECTION 5. LOYALTY.

A trustee shall invest and manage the trust assets solely in the interests of the beneficiaries.

SECTION 6. IMPARTIALITY.

If a trust has two or more beneficiaries, the trustee shall act impartially in investing and managing the trust assets, taking into account any differing interests of the beneficiaries.

SECTION 7. INVESTMENT COSTS.

In investing and managing trust assets, a trustee may only incur costs that are appropriate and reasonable in relation to the assets, the purposes of the trust, and the skills of the trustee.

SECTION 8.   REVIEWING COMPLIANCE.

Compliance with the prudent investor rule is determined in light of the facts and circumstances existing at the time of a trustee's decision or action and not by hindsight.

SECTION 9. DELEGATION OF INVESTMENT AND MANAGEMENT FUNCTIONS.

(a)   A trustee may delegate investment and management functions that a prudent trustee of comparable skills could properly delegate under the circumstances. The trustees shall exercise reasonable care, skill and caution in:

(1) selecting an agent;

(2) establishing the scope and terms of the delegation, consistent with the purposes and terms of the trust; and

(3) periodically reviewing the agent's actions in order to monitor the agent's performance and compliance with the terms of the delegation.

(b) In performing a delegated function, an agent owes a duty to the trust to exercise reasonable care to comply with the terms of the delegation.

(c) who complies with the requirements of subsection (a) is not liable to the beneficiaries or to the trust for the decisions or actions of the agent to whom the function was delegated.

(d) By accepting the delegation of a trust's function from the trustee of a trust that is subject to the law of this state, an agent submits to the jurisdiction of the courts of this state.

SECTION 10. LANGUAGE INVOKING STANDARD OF [ACT].

The following terms or comparable language in the provisions of a trust, unless otherwise limited or modified, authorizes any investment or strategy permitted under this [Act]: "investment permissible by law for investment of trust funds," "legal investments," " authorized investments." "using the judgment and care under the circumstances then prevailing that persons of prudence, discretion, and intelligence exercise in the management of their own affairs, not in regard to speculation but in regard to the permanent disposition of their own funds, considering the probable income as well as the probable safety of their capital," "prudent man rule," prudent trustee rule," prudent person rule,' and "prudent investor rule."

SECTION 11. APPLICATION TO EXISTING TRUSTS. This [Act] applies to trusts existing on and created after its effective date. As applied to trusts existing on its effective date, this [Act] governs only decisions or actions occurring after that date.

SECTION 12. UNIFORMITY OF APPLICATION AND CONSTRUCTION. This [Act] shall be applied and construed to effectuate its general purpose to make uniform the law with respect to the subject of the [Act] among the States enacting it.

SECTION 13. SHORT TITLE This [Act] may be cited as "[name of Enacting State] Uniform Prudent Investor Act."

SECTION 14. SEVERABILITY. If any provision of this [Act] or its application to any person or circumstances is held invalid, the invalidity does not affect other provisions or application of this [Act] which can be given effect without the invalid provision or application, and to this and the provisions of this [Act] are severable.

SECTION 15. EFFECTIVE DATE. This [Act] takes effect . . . .

States that have Adopted this new Uniform Act

Alaska	Nebraska
Arizona	New Hampshire
Arkansas	New Jersey
California	New Mexico
Colorado	North Carolina
Connecticut	North Dakota
District of Columbia	Ohio
Hawaii	Oklahoma
Idaho	Oregon
Illinois	Pennsylvania
Indiana	Rhode Island
Iowa	Utah
Kansas	Vermont
Maine	Virginia
Massachusetts	Washington
Michigan	West Virginia
Minnesota	Wyoming
Missouri	

Note:

Some states have adopted this Act with changes. As examples: Florida adopted the Act with a change that makes the professional entity selected a "Trustee." Maryland has adopted an Act that is substantially similar.

instead of the position of an Agent" [6] as stated in the Act. Your Trust attorney can advise you of the status of this Act in your State.

Additional information on this Act and the "Uniform Principal and Income Act [1997][7] can be obtained from:

National Conference of Commissioners
On Uniform State Laws
211 E. Ontario Street, Suite 1300
Chicago, Illinois 60611
312/915-0195

(6)   See Section 9 of the ACT

(7)   Does not address the options contained in this book. But, does state that the Grantor can override the Act.

Information for Completing
Exhibit 1 & 2
"INCOME NEEDS OF EACH SPOUSE"

Introduction

Completing this worksheet is not meant to be an exhaustive time-consuming operation. Reasonable estimates can be made and placed in the various sections. It is better that more income rather than less be available for the surviving spouse, so it is best to err on the high side.

The example of a completed worksheet for both husband and wife on pages 52 and 53 combined their individual needs onto one form to show that each of them required a different income from the Trust.   In this case, the wife needed an additional $18,000 a year from the trust (see page 53).

Separate worksheet for each person

Separate worksheets should be prepared for each person since their individual income and assets will be different.   Exhibit 1 on Page 52 assumed that each person would have the same amount of stocks, mutual funds, bonds, CDs and Saving Accounts totaling $785,000 after the death of their spouse. The assets are not likely to be the same, and that is another reason why a separate form must be prepared for each person.

Exhibit 1 - Insert the name of the person for whom this form is being prepared.

A. ANNUAL INCOME NEEDED

before Income Taxes excluding the cost of a new car, vacations and other items listed in Exhibit 2.

$ _____

This is generally your total gross income on your tax return for last year. No attempt is made at the start of this process to reduce current income needs resulting from the death of a spouse. Planning to immediately move after the first spouse dies to reduce your expenses can be a mistake.

If your income was less than needed last year and you did any of the following:

Borrowed money, increased your credit card balances, or used any of your savings or investments these amounts should be added to last year's income to obtain an accurate total of your income needs.

A-2 . SOURCES OF INCOME excluding Trust:

a. Social Security $ _____

For husband, enter the amount you are currently receiving. The wife, in most cases, should contact the local Social Security office to obtain an estimate of what she would receive as the surviving spouse. It can be about 80% of the amount their deceased spouse was paid.

b. Pensions $ _____

If you are working now, do not include this income. If your current position has retirement benefits and you will receive these, enter that amount. If your spouse receives a pension, enter the amount, if any, you would receive after their death.

c. IRAs; 401k, etc. $ _____

This section needs to be carefully reviewed. Certain types of retirement plans require withdrawals starting after age 70. Others, such as a Roth IRA, do not require withdrawals. As a first estimate, you could consider removing three or four percent a year, especially if you need income.

A-2, c   Other: List by type

	Current value	Income
- Stocks & Mutual Funds	$ _____	$ _____
- Bonds	$ _____	$ _____
- CDs & Saving Account	$ _____	$ _____
- Other - Life Insurance	$ _____	$ _____
TOTALS	$	$

<u>The above section requires some careful thought as to which assets are in the name of the other spouse in order to qualify for the Credit Shelter Trust.</u> If your home, stocks, other securities, mutual funds, etc. are in joint names with right of survivorship, they will pass directly to the surviving spouse. Therefore these items will appear on each person's form.

For an asset to be placed in your Credit Shelter Trust ,the asset must be in your name. Therefore these assets will remain on your form but will not be on your spouse's form. They will be in your Credit Shelter Trust or Marital Trust and be the source of income for your income beneficiary.

TOTAL INCOME $ _____
PRIOR TO ADDITIONAL SPECIAL
NEEDS as shown on Exhibit 2.

This is the total of all expected sources of income shown above - Social Security, pension, IRAs, stocks, bonds and other investments and holdings.

Status of Income Prior to
Special Needs:
Subtract **"Total Sources of Income"** from **"A"** above, **"Annual Income Needed."**
 Annual Income Needed ("A") $_____
Less: Total Sources of Income ("B") -$_____
Shortage or Surplus of Income
Prior to Special Needs (Exhibit 2) (+/-) $ _____

Exhibit 2 - Insert the name of the person this form is being prepared for. The husband and the wife should each have a separate form.

B.   Estimated Annual Expenses
      For special needs:

Note: These expenses are listed on an after-tax basis since most of us consider the cost of cars, vacations, repairs, gift, etc. as the actual cost of these items.

B-1   Replacement Car costing $ _____
       Divided by _____ years = $ _____
       On Page 53 a replacement car costing $20,000, after trade-in of the old car, was used with an estimated life of four years. This resulted in an annual cost, over the estimated four-year life, of $5,000.

B-2 Provision for major home maintenance
and replacement of appliances $ _____

If you own a home, maintenance, roof repairs and replacement must be expected. You will need to set up an annual reserve for these types of items.

B-3 Gifts and assistance to Children and
Grandchildren $ _____

<u>This section requires thoughtful consideration.</u>. In addition to gifts for birthdays and holidays, are there now or might there be in the future special needs to assist your children or grandchildren that you would like to provide for? If you will have high estates taxes, after the death of your spouse, will you make use of annual gifts of $10,000 to any or all members of your family? Do you plan to pay for the education of any of your grandchildren ,etc.? If so, include these amounts here.

B-4 Travel & Vacations $ _____

If you visit your children and grandchildren, travel with friends, etc., enter the total costs of these trips including meals and lodging, airline tickets, car rentals, etc.

B-5 Other Special Needs: List $ _____

B-6 AFTER TAX TOTAL $ _____

Note: In this section the calculation is made to determine the pre-income tax cost of the above items. This provides for the added income

**required to pay state and federal income taxes on
these additional expenses.**

Example: If all of the additional expenses in Section B
total $15,000 and your top tax bracket is 35% for both
state and federal taxes, increase the $15,000 by 54% or
$ 8,077. Stated another way: A Taxable Income of
$23,077 at a 35% tax rate nets $15,000 that you can
spend.

    INCREASE _____% = $ _____

B-6 . PRE-TAX TOTAL of Special Needs $ _____

FROM EXHIBIT 1:
Shortage(+) or Surplus (-) of Income
Prior to Special Needs   (+/-) $ _____

Note: It is very important that the proper value of the
income be placed here from Exhibit 1. As a guide, if the
"Sources of Income" on Exhibit 1 are less than your
income needs, then you have a shortage of income. This
shortage must be added to your other needs in Exhibit
2 to determine your total needs from the Trust.

    If there is a surplus of income from Exhibit 1,
this surplus amount is subtracted from your additional
needs in Exhibit 2.

C.   TOTAL ANNUAL INCOME
REQUIRED FROM TRUST IN
YEAR IT IS EXECUTED (D. + E.) $ _____

Special Notes:

    1. Using this method to determine the income required from the Trust, the amount entered in item "C" is entered in the Trust as the amount to be paid the year the Trust was executed. And directives in the Trust, to increase this amount annually for inflation starting in the year the trust was executed, should be given.

    2. If the amount in item C is over 5% of the value of the Trust, serious consideration should be given to new sources of additional income, such as the proceeds from life insurance policies.

    3. If the above amount is over $19,000, you need to consider revising your estate planning documents if they are silent as to the income to be paid for the surviving spouse from the Credit Shelter Trust. This is discussed in Chapter 7. There are other important options that can be considered that are presented in this book.

ALSO NOTE:

THE SURVIVING SPOUSE SHOULD HAVE AMPLE FUNDS AVAILABLE. AND, IF POSSIBLE HAVE SUFFICIENT FUNDS FOR GIFTS AND NEEDS OF CHILDREN AND GRANDCHILDREN. THE GOAL IS TO MAINTAIN A STRONG FAMILY RELATIONSHIP.

How To Use Your Internet Estate Planning Programs

Introduction:

These Programs were developed for CPAs and financial planners who assist clients in estate planning. However, many grantors who have computers and like to use them for financial information and investing will find the Programs of value for their own estate planning concerns.

The calculations for each Program use simple mathematical factors such as percent, plus and minus. Before you start using the data and calculations loaded into your computer, check the validity of the transferred data by manually checking the Program. There is always the possibility that what was downloaded from the Internet may have been in error or that there are problems in your computer.

To do this, check the results expected by randomly selecting the factors that are used to obtain the results. Check your answers against those in the Program. The math functions for each Estate Planning Program are explained in this appendix.

Another benefit from this data checking exercise is that you will understand the interrelationship of the data used as input for each program.

There are two different Estate Planning Programs that you can access at the web site, " www.ccmtrust.com/thebook" Each one has a special purpose explained in this section. You will need to have installed in your computer Microsoft Excel Version 5.0 or higher.

After you have downloaded the Programs and the instruction sheets into your computer, it will no longer be necessary for you to remain connected to the Internet. If you do not have a computer or access to the Internet, ask a friend who does to run these Programs for you. You can also use the computers at your library, senior center, or other community organizations. Generally, there are people at these locations who can assist you.

Changing one or more of the planning assumptions at the top of each Program will allow you to test many different alternatives and to select the ones you want to consider for your Trust. You can print out the results of each test.

INSTRUCTION FOR EACH OF THE ESTATE PLANNING CALCULATORS.

Estate Planning Program One

The design of this Program allows you to select the starting income your spouse or other income beneficiary will require. The starting income was obtained by using Exhibits 1 and 2 - Income Needs of each Spouse. The Program allows you to annually increase the income for inflation by a stated percentage; to select and test various combinations of investments in bonds and stocks; to assign reasonable forecasts of interest paid on bonds and dividends that might be expected from stocks. Based on your forecast of the average annual increase in stocks, you can view the expected results of different rates of growth. The Program is based on the following ten planning assumptions.

Starting Income Required	**$ XX,XXX**	**Starting Year**	**XXXX**
Annual Increase	**X.X%**	**Percent in Stocks**	**XX.X%**
Starting Value of Trust	**$ XXX,XXX**	**Annual Increase**	**XX.X%**
Percent in Bonds	**XX.X%**	**Stock Dividends**	**X.X%**
Bond Interest	**X.X%**	**Trust Fees**	
		& Expenses	**X.XX%**

Explanations of items that are used as input into the program, calculations made by the Program, and examples of expected results are given at web site "www.ccmtrust.com/the book.

Once you have entered the above estate planning factors into the Program, the results are quickly calculated by very simple addition, subtraction and percentages. The results are printed for you. There may seem to be a large amount of data presented, but a review of the calculations made for the first year will help you to understand and test the results.

The results indicate the <u>Annual Income</u> that can be paid from the Credit Shelter Trust over a twenty-five year period, based on your planning assumptions. The Programs can be extended on twenty-five year increments by entering as new data the resulting amounts at the end of the twenty-fifth year. This new data will be the starting point for calculating the expected results over the second twenty-year period.

As you enter data, always ask yourself "What would happen if their was a major decline in the stock market and especially immediately after my death?" You can make estimates of this and suggestions for doing it are included in the material from our web site.

Use Estate Planning Program One for Second Marriage Trusts

In Chapter 12 second marriage Trusts were discussed. An example was shown of the funds required to be placed in a Trust for Margaret Bright, who would need an income of $24,135 in 2001 dollars. The table on Page 116, indicated that her husband could obtain that income for her with $500,000 placed in a Trust in 2001. The amount was obtained using Estate Planning Program One.

CAUTION: Remember these amounts are forecasted estimates. Hopefully they are made conservatively. It is your best judgement coupled with a planning tool. But there is no guarantee for any forecast.

Estate Planning Program Two

This program is used for a Grantor who wants the end-value of their Credit Shelter Trust to grow for the maximum benefit of the children and other heirs. This Program does not require either of these two planning factors: "Starting Income From Trust" or "Annual Increase" in the starting income.

Listed with the instructions available from our web site are the planning factors that you can change each time you run this Program. The explanation for "Starting Value of the Trust," "Percent in Bonds,"

"Percent in Stocks," "Interest on Bonds," Dividend Percent" and "Annual Growth in Stocks" are the same as those in Estate Planning Program One. You can review the use of each starting on our web site and the simple mathematical calculations that are used.

Starting Value	**$ XXX,XXX**	**Bonds Interest**	**XX,X%**
Percent in Bonds	**XX.X%**	**Stock Dividends**	**X.X%**
Percent In Stocks	**XX.X%**	**Trustee Fees &**	
Annual Growth		**Expenses**	**X.X%**
in Stocks	**XX%**	**Charged to Income**	**X.X%**

Estate Planning Program Two does contain a new planning factor, your option of a Directive on the Trustee Fees. You can determine if they are to be charges against the <u>Income</u> of the Trust or charged against the <u>principal</u> of the Trust. If you want to view the results of a Net Income provision in a Trust, charge half of the Trustee Fees and Expenses to income.

If you want to increase the value of the Trust for your children, you can give a directive to charge all of the <u>Trustees Fees and Expenses</u> to income. To do this, use the exact same percentage of <u>Trustee Tees and Expenses</u> and enter it as <u>Charged to Income</u> .

NOTE:

The Estate Planning Programs and the calculations that result used in this book are for instructional purposes only. Any calculations obtained need to be independently verified if they are to be used in actual estate planning.

"A" AND "B" TRUST or "A/B" TRUST: See Credit Shelter Trust.

ACCOUNTING PERIOD: A calendar year unless a different 12-month period is selected.

ADVANCEMENT: An amount of funds or other type of assets given to an heir during the lifetime of that person, intended as an advance against the future heir's share of the estate.

ANNUAL EXCLUSION: Up to $10,000. per year that a person is allowed to give to another person without having to pay a gift tax. Married couples can give up to $20,000 per year. The amount allowed is being indexed to inflation.

ATTORNEY in FACT: Your agent given authorization by you to represent you and to take certain actions on your behalf. This should be in writing and for some acts, may require notarization.

BENEFICIARY: A person named in your Will or Trust to receive gifts. A Trust refers to such persons as an income beneficiary and a remainder beneficiary (generally called the remaindermen).An organization can also be named as a beneficiary.

BEQUEST: Property transferred under your Will.

BYPASS TRUST: See Credit Shelter Trust.

CAPITAL: The value of an asset. Referred to as principal in Trusts.

CASE LAW: Laws established by court decisions.

CHARITABLE REMAINDER UNITRUST: The donation of assets to a Trust in which you receive a lifetime income. You may name a second recipient, such as a child to also receive this lifetime income after your death. Has great tax advantages. See Chapter 18.

CHARITABLE TRUST: A Trust created for a charitable purpose as described in the Internal Revenue Code.

CODICIL: An amendment to a Will. It must be as properly executed as the Will.

COMMUNITY PROPERTY: Property acquired by a husband and wife during their marriage and subject to special laws in several states.

CONSERVATOR: A person appointed by a court to, administer the estate of a minor or adult individual.

CORPORATE TRUSTEE: An organization such as a bank that acts as trustee.

CO-TENANCY: When two or more parties own the same property and it remains undivided.

CO-TRUSTEE: Two or more individuals serving as trustee, or a family member serving with a corporate trustee /professional trustee.

CREDIT SHELTER TRUST: A Trust established to retain your federal-estate tax exemption for your heirs, $675,000 in 2001 and increasing to $1 million in 2006, while providing your income beneficiary with income and other benefits during his or her lifetime. A Credit Shelter Trust is sometimes referred to by other names.

DECEDENT: A term used for the person who died.

DEFAULT RULES: When your Trust is silent on any of the financial and management options, the state will determine each of these options such as how the funds will be invested. You may not want your Trust controlled by many of the Default Rules. See Appendix C and other references to Default Rules in the book.

DEVISE: Real Estate that is transferred under a Will.

DIRECTIVE: An instruction given by the grantor as to what is to be done, such as "I direct my trustee to pay my surviving spouse $35,000 a year starting on the date this Trust is executed and to increased this amount annually for inflation.

DISCLAIMER: If an heir does not wish to accept all or part of a bequest, they may disclaim it. If the disclaimer is made within the required time, it can be made without tax consequences.

DOMICILE: The place a person permanently resides.

DURABLE POWER OF ATTORNEY : A legal document in which you give a person(s) the authority to handle your financial matters. If you become disabled, a Durable Power of Attorney will continue to be valid. See page 144 of Chapter 17.

ESTATE TAX: A tax that the states and federal government place on your assets at the time of your death. Currently the federal estate tax applies to estates with a market value of over $675,000 and this increases to $1 million in 2006. State taxes on estates and exemptions vary by state. See Chapter 18, on "Removing Assets from Your Estate to Reduce Taxes.

EXECUTOR (the male form) : **EXECUTRIX** (the female form): A person named by you in your Last Will and Testament" to account for all your assets, pay your expenses, just debts and taxes, and to distribute your assets to your beneficiaries and/or trustee according to the terms of your Will and any other documents.

EXEMPTION TRUST: See Credit Shelter Trust.

FAMILY BUSINESS: Major ownership of a business. Many times there is a limited market for the shares of ownership. May qualify for an additional tax exemption.

FEDERAL ESTATE TAX EXEMPTION: The amount each individual's estate that is exempt from federal estate taxes. This amount is $675,000 in 2001 and is scheduled to increase to one million dollars in 2006. A husband and wife can combine their individual federal estate tax exemption to shelter $1,350,000 in 2001 and two million dollars in 2006. Properly prepared legal documents are required to obtain this combined exemption.

FIDUCIARY: A person in a position of financial and other types of responsibility. The person may be the executor of your Will; the Trustee of your Trust; a Personal Representative or a Guardian. See duties in Appendix B.

GENERATION-SKIPPING TRANSFER TAX: A special tax assessed on transfers in excess of $1 million to anyone two generations below the grantor, such as grandchildren and great grandchildren.

GIFT: Transfer of an asset without requiring payment of any type.

GRANTOR: (Also called a **Trustor, Donor, Settlor, Testator, Creator).** An individual who forms the Trust and transfers assets into the Trust. The transfer of assets into the Trust can be done at any time - while the grantor is living or at their death. Proper legal documentation is required.

GROSS INCOME PROVISION: Provides that all of the fees to manage the Trust and expenses are to be paid out of the principal of the Trust. The income beneficiary receives all of the income from the Trust. A Gross Income provision provides for a greater income paid to the surviving spouse or other income beneficiaries. See Chapter 7.

GUARDIAN: A person appointed by a court to make decisions regarding the support, care, education, health and welfare of a minor or adult individual.

GUARDIANSHIP: The responsibility for a minor or a person requiring special care.

HEALTH CARE POWER OF ATTORNEY A legal document in which you give another person the power to make medical decisions if you are unable to do so. See Page 144 of Chapter 17

HEIRS: The persons who are to receive the assets after your death..

INCOME: Interest paid on Bonds, CDs and other securities generally called "Fixed Income Investments" and dividends paid on equities. Can include income a Trustee receives from a Trust asset, such as real estate.

INCOME BENEFICIARY: Generally your spouse. This is the person who will receive income from the Trust and (if properly stated in your Trust) should be able to receive additional funds from the principal of the Trust. NOTE: This person has no authority to change how the assets will be distributed upon this or her death unless provided for in a Directive you as the grantor can give. See Chapter 8.

INCOMPETENT: An individual who ha been declared by a court to be unable to handle and manage their own affairs.

INSURANCE TRUST: See Irrevocable Life Insurance Trust in Chapter 18.

INTER VIVOS TRUST: See "Living Trust"

INTESTATE: A person who dies without a Will or any other device to transfer their property.

INVASION OF PRINCIPAL: This is an act of taking funds from the principal of the Trust for the benefit of one or more of the beneficiaries of the Trust. Special instructions are in the Trust that indicate the conditions upon which the trustee will take funds from the principal of your trust for the benefit of your spouse or others. See Chapter 9.

INVESTMENT CLASSIFICATIONS OF TRUSTS: The right a grantor of a Trust has to state how the assets of a Trust will be invested. If the grantor of a Trust states that 100% of the assets of a Trust will be invested in good quality medium-term bonds or 100% invested in stocks (and these instructions may include the type of stocks, or any other percentage combination) the trustee must follow these instructions. But if the Trust is silent on this or any other key rights a grantor has, then "Default Rules" will be followed.

IRREVOCABLE: A Trust a grantor establishes that cannot be changed once it has been executed.

JOINT TENANCY WITH RIGHT OF SURVIVORSHIP: A legal form of ownership used by many husbands and wives for assets they own together and in which the title is in both of their names with the right of the survivor to fully own the property such as real estate (their homes) and their securities. The tax consequences of this type of ownership is not properly understood by many people.

NOTE: Assets held in "Joint Tenancy with Right of Survivorship" cannot be placed into a Credit Shelter Trust. As an example, if your home is held in your name and your spouse's name as "Joint tenancy with right of survivorship" you have already, by a legally recorded document, willed your ownership interest directly to your surviving spouse or to anyone else with whom you jointly held the property . Therefore, you cannot remove this prior ownership agreement by now placing your ownership of the real estate or brokerage account into your Credit Shelter Trust. There is an exception for assets owned with your spouse if your Will or "Living Trust" has a disclaimer provision in it. But this is not generally recommended.

LIVING TRUSTS: A type of Trust established to avoid probate, See Chapter 26

LIVING WILL: A legal document in which you generally state that you choose a natural death; you do not want your life maintained by artificial means and in it you also have the option of stating several other key items of medical care that you want or do not want. See Chapter 17.

MARITAL DEDUCTION: Any amount of assets given to a spouse are exempt from estate taxes. But, if the surviving spouse's estate is more than the federal estate tax exemption, estate taxes will become payable.

MARITAL LIFE ESTATE TRUST: See Marital Trust and Chapter 14.

MARITAL TRUST: To control other assets you pass tax-free to your surviving spouse. See Chapter 14.

MINOR: A person who under state law is not old enough to be considered an adult.

NET INCOME PROVISION: 50% of the annual trustee fees and expenses are charged against the gross income of the Trust, The other 50% is charged against the principal. This reduces the income that the Income Beneficiary will receive by about 10%. See Chapter 13.

PAYABLE-ON-DEATH: An account designation for assets such as bank accounts and brokerage accounts that will transfer the assets held to the person named as beneficiary. Several terms are used for these types of accounts. The most common is the "TOD" account ("Transfer On Death"). Assets so designated escape probate but not estate taxes.

PER CAPITA: A distribution from an estate made equally to a class of people such as grandchildren

PERPETUITIES, RULES AGAINST: Federal Tax law which restricts the numbers of year assets may be held in a Trust. Generally a Trust can last during the entire lifetime of someone who is alive when the Trust was established and for an additional 21 years. This restriction does not apply to Charitable Trusts. For more detailed information, consult your attorney.

PERSONAL PROPERTY: Generally possessions that can be moved. Cash, Savings accounts, Stocks and bonds, Furniture, automobiles, equipment, stamp and coin collections, guns, etc,

PER STIRPES: A distribution from an estate made equally among family lines. As an example, if the Grantor had three children, the funds would follow the family line. Therefore, grandchildren could receive more than if the distribution had been made per capita or less.

PLANNED INCOME TRUST: This is the most important type of Trust to consider. The Trust is prepared by first considering the annual amount the income beneficiary will need from the Trust. These income needs are determined in today's dollars and entered into the Trust with an annual increase from that date forward for inflation. And, since official government figures do not adequately provide for senior citizens' needs, an annual minimum increase of 3% is recommended. A second option is to provide a surviving spouse with the power to instruct the trustee to distribute income to the children and other heirs named by the grantor in the document.

If and when the value of the Trust exceeds an amount designated by the grantor, there is a third option. It provides a surviving spouse with the power to instruct the trustee to distribute principal to the children and other heirs named by the grantor in the document. Other important options to consider are presented in this book

POUR-OVER WILL: See Chapter 17.

PRINCIPAL: Assets held by the trustee for distribution to the remainder beneficiaries when the Trust is terminated.

PROBATE: A court procedure that all of your assets not excluded by other documents will pass through. Among the several key things that probate does is to change title of your assets from your name to those you have named in your Will, if you had one. In probate your executor is appointed, generally the person you have named in your Will. Your debts are to be paid and states require that advertisements are to be placed many times in newspapers announcing your death and asking that any debts you owe be submitted by a certain date. Other issues are concluded prior to the distribution of your estate to your heirs. Many people use a"Living Trust" and other means to avoid the delays of probate and to keep their assets and other information from becoming part of the public record. See Chapter 16.

REMAINDERMEN: Generally your children. These are the individuals named in your Trust who are to receive the assets in your Trust after the death of either the income beneficiary or other person(s) receiving the income no longer do so because that right was terminated by other conditions in your Trust.

REVOCABLE TRUST: See Living Trusts.

RULE AGAINST PERPETUITIES: The law that voids a future interest in property if the transfer will take effect within a stated period of time. Generally the period is the lifetime of a person, living when the Trust became effective plus an additional 21 years.

SETTLOR: A person who establishes a Trust. See Grantor.

SILENT: A legal term meaning that the document neglected to state what was to be done. In these cases the issues may be decided by what are called Default Rules. Each State has their own set of Default Rules.

SPENDTHRIFT PROVISION: a directive of a Trust which restrains both the voluntary and involuntary transfer of a beneficiary's interest.

SPOUSAL BYPASS TRUST: See Credit Shelter Trust.

SPRINKLING POWER: A directive in a Trust that gives sole authority to the trustee to determine how the income from the Trust and the principal may be given to different Trust beneficiaries or retained in the Trust. A grantor should consider giving this authority to the surviving spouse, instead of the trustee. See option Chapter 8.

STEPPED-UP BASIS This is a tax term the meaning and use of which is important to understand. When a person dies, his or her assets are "Marked-to Market."

In the case of listed securities, the newspapers report daily the current values. Appraisals are also made on other types of property such as the value of the real estate owned, objects of art, etc.

These are values "Stepped-up" from their original costs. These "Stepped-up" values will be used for tax purposes. It is the value of the items you can place into your $675,000 Bypass Trust in 2001 . And, missed by many in estate planning, it is the tax base of all assets given to your wife who receives these tax free. An example is if you left your wife stocks with a low cost value to you, these stocks will now have a "Stepped-up" value (the market) and your wife could sell these with no capital gain taxes. This could be a good time to sell these stocks and instruct your spouse to invest in a better diversified holding such as mutual funds and index funds.

SUCCESSOR TRUSTEE: When the prior trustee is unable to serve, a person designated in a Trust to replace the original trustee or another successor trustee.

TENANCY IN COMMON: Two or more people own the same property and there is no right of survivorship. Therefore a deceased person's share passes to their estate.

TESTAMENTARY TRUST: A Trust that is established at your death generally under your Last Will and Testament. The most common example is the Credit Shelter Trust that uses the $ 675,000 federal estate tax exemption(in 2001) for each individual.

TOTAL RETURN TRUST: An attempt to find a formula approach to solve the income needs of a spouse or other income beneficiary by investing 100% of the trust assets in stocks. The annual income from this type of Trust fluctuates with the ups and downs of the stock market. A "Total Return Trust" violates the first principal of estate planning: to provide for the income beneficiary a steady dependable income adjusted for inflation. For information on providing a steady dependable income, see Chapter 7.

TOTAL RETURN UNITRUST: Another name for a "Total Return Trust" described above. Presents serious estate planning problems. The major problem is that the income paid changes with the market and that income can fall below the amount needed. Other key options may also be missing.

TRUST: A document that provides for assets to be held and managed by a person or entity, such as a bank, called the trustee. The trustee manages these assets according to the terms of the Trust.

TRUST ASSETS: These can be in any form, cash, securities, property, etc. These are transferred to your Trust to be managed by your trustee for the benefits and objectives stated in your Trust documentation. Remember, if your trust is silent on any of the options and objectives of your Trust, state "Default Rules" will then determine how these assets are invested along with other important issues that you had neglected to address..

TRUSTEE: The person or organization that will manage your Trust. Be sure to name successor trustees in case the person named initially is not able to serve. If you fail to name successor trustees, the court will name them. These could be people you would not choose and would not want as your trustee. Put directives in your Trust that allow your income beneficiary or others to replace the trustee and successor trustee and name a new trustee. See Chapter 9.

UNIFIED CREDIT: A federal exemption from federal estate taxes that every person is entitled to obtain. Currently the value of the Unified Credit is $675,000 in 2001 and increases to $1 million in 2006. A Credit Shelter Trust was designed to make maximum use of this unified credit so that a husband and wife can shelter assets up to $2 million in 2006. By doing so, they can save $235,000 or more in estate taxes. The tax credit can be applied toward gifts and that part of the remaining unified credit not used during a person's lifetime, can then be used for estate taxes.

UNIFIED CREDIT SHELTER TRUST: See Credit Shelter Trust.

UNIFORM TRANSFER TO MINORS ACT (UTMA): Assets placed in this type of account pass to a person when they reach the legal age, generally 18. Better alternatives to a UTMA are presented in this book such as a gift Trust, see page 151.

WILL: A document that should be properly prepared with the assistance of an attorney in the state of your residence in order to conform to the laws of that state. This document appoints an executor of your estate and successor executors if the initial person so named is unable to serve.. It states how your assets are to be distributed and if there are beneficiaries who are minors, it names a trustee or guardian of the funds you gave to minors. It may name the trustee and successor trustees for special Trusts you established such as a Credit Shelter Trust and the terms and conditions for investing, managing, and making payments from the Trust.

Exhibit 1   241

INCOME NEEDS OF EACH SPOUSE

Name of Person _____

**A. ANNUAL INCOME NEEDED
before Income Taxes**. Excluding
the cost of a new car and other
items listed in Exhibit 2. $ _____

**B. SOURCES OF INCOME
   excluding Trust:**
    a. Social Security $ _____
    b. Pensions $ _____
    c. IRAs, 401k, etc. $ _____
       Sub total $

B. - d. Other: List by type,

	Current Value	Income
- Stocks & Mutual Funds	$ _____	$ _____
- Bonds	$ _____	$ _____
- CDs & Saving Account	$ _____	$ _____
TOTALS	$	$

B - TOTAL- SOURCES OF INCOME $ _____
**PRIOR TO ADDITIONAL
SPECIAL NEEDS, SUCH AS:**
 - Provision for replacement car
 - Major home maintenance &
  Replacement of appliances
- Gifts & assistance to Children
- Travel & Vacations

SUMMARY:
Annual Income Needed ("A" above) $ _____
Less Total Sources of Income ("B" above) - $ _____
**Shortage or Surplus of income Prior
to Special Needs (Exhibit 2)** $ _____

Exhibit 2

243

INCOME NEEDS OF EACH SPOUSE
FROM THE TRUST

Name of Person _____

**C. Estimated Annual Expenses
For special needs:**

C-1 Replacement Car costing $ _____
divided by ____ years = $ _____

C-2 Provision for Major home
maintenance & Replacement
of appliances $ _____

C-3 Gifts & assistance to Children
and grandchildren $ _____

C-4 Travel & Vacations $ _____

C-5 Other Special Needs - List $ _____

C-6 AFTER TAX TOTAL $ _____

Convert After Tax Total needed for special
needs to an amount prior to federal and state
income taxes: If your top tax bracket is 20%,
increase by 25%; if your top tax bracket is
25%, increase by 33%; if your top tax bracket
is 30%, increase by 43%; if your top tax
bracket is 37% increase by 59%.

INCREASE ____% = $ _____

D. PRE-TAX TOTAL of Special Needs $

E. FROM EXHIBIT 1:
Shortage (+) or Surplus (-) of income
Prior to Special Needs   (+/-) $ _____

F. TOTAL ANNUAL INCOME
REQUIRED FROM TRUST IN
YEAR IT IS EXECUTED (D.+E.) $ _____

*NOTE: Amount placed in trust must be increased for
inflation starting from the date of the trust.*

NOTE: Under the last column entitled "Include" indicate by a check mark if you want this option in your documents. An asterisk (*) next to an option number indicates that I recommend including it.

OPTIONS FOR:

A. My Spouse's Income:

Option	Description	Include
1.*	Annual Income to be paid to my surviving spouse: Starting amount this year $ _____ Increased for inflation	
2. *	My spouse has complete authority to obtain an additional $5,000 each year from the trust.	
3. *	Additional funds required from the trust will be paid at sole discretion of my trustee.	

B. My Spouse is to be the head of the Family

Option	Description	Include
4.*	My spouse can instruct my trustee to distribute income to my children.	
5. *	My spouse can instruct my trustee to distribute principal to my children	
6. *	To protect my spouse from excessive distributions from principal, I establish amounts below which distributions can not be made.	

B. My Spouse to be the head of the Family (continued)

Option	Description	Include

Option	Description	Include
7. A	When distributions of income are made, they are to be made in equal amounts to all my children, **OR**	
7. B*	Distribution of unequal amounts of income to my children is permitted.	
8. *	Up to 50% of the actual income received by the Trust can be distributed to my children upon the written instructions of my spouse without decreasing payments of my spouse's income. Distributions to my children over 50% of the actual income will reduce dollar for dollar the income my spouse is to receive that year.	
9. A *	When distributions of principal are made, they are to be made in equal amounts to all my children, **OR**	
9. B	Distribution of unequal amounts of principal to my children is permitted.	
10. *	My spouse shall have the right to direct that a beneficiary's share of income or principal from this Trust be held in Trust under terms and condition my spouse indicates. This includes a beneficiary's share upon my spouse's death.	
11.	My surviving spouse shall have the right to change the share each child and heir will receive upon my spouse's death.	

C. Family visits

Option	Description	Include
12.*	Trust is to pay reasonable travel expenses for visits by my children to my spouse when ill or in a nursing home.	
13.*	Trust shall also pay travel expenses for our Grandchildren's visits to my spouse.	
14. *	Trust to pay travel expenses for our children to attend spouse's funeral.	
15. *	My spouse shall have the authority to remove the trustee and appoint a new one.	

D. Trustee & Safeguarding Assets

Option	Description	Include
16.*	All assets in my Trust will be held by a bank acting as custodian or in a brokerage account.	
17. *	Copies of all reports of the custodian or brokerage firm are to be sent to my trustee and all my beneficiaries	
18. *	My trustee can change custodian or brokerage firm.	
19. *	All transfers of assets from custodians or brokerage houses are to be made directly to new custodian or broker.	

E. Trust   Investments and Payments

Option	Description	Include
20. *	The initial investments of my Trust are as follows: Stocks_____%; Bonds_____%	
21. *	As stocks increase in value, do not sell them and buy bonds to re-balance my portfolio.	
22. *	Payments from principal are to be made from the proceeds of stock sales.	

F.   Imporatant Options to Include

Option	Description	Include
23. *	Ability to change the state that controls my Trust.	
24*	Include here the special needs of your family such as particular requirements for individual members, providing for special events, anticipating the unplanned or the unusual happenings that can occur in the lifetime of the family.	

Review some of the items in Chapter 11, such as <u>Anticipating probable needs</u> on page 108. Review any items you marked and notes you made as you read this book.

Remember, it is your money, you can control its future use. A key objective in all of your documents is to encourage the continuation of strong family relationships.